THE
RICHEST MAN IN BABYLON

IN TEN MINUTES A DAY

THE
RICHEST MAN
IN BABYLON

IN TEN MINUTES A DAY

**DAILY WISDOM TO BUILD WEALTH
AND FINANCIAL FREEDOM**

George S. Clason

© Copyright 2025– George S. Clason

All rights reserved. This book is protected by the copyright laws of the United States of America. No part of this publication may be reproduced, stored in or introduced into a retrieval system, or transmitted, in any form or by any means (electronic, mechanical, photocopying, recording or otherwise), without the prior written permission of the publisher. For permissions requests, contact the publisher, addressed "Attention: Permissions Coordinator," at the address below.

Published and distributed by:

SOUND WISDOM
P.O. Box 310
Shippensburg, PA 17257-0310

717-530-2122

info@soundwisdom.com

www.soundwisdom.com

While efforts have been made to verify information contained in this publication, neither the author nor the publisher assumes any responsibility for errors, inaccuracies, or omissions. While this publication is chock-full of useful, practical information; it is not intended to be legal or accounting advice. All readers are advised to seek competent lawyers and accountants to follow laws and regulations that may apply to specific situations. The reader of this publication assumes responsibility for the use of the information. The author and publisher assume no responsibility or liability whatsoever on the behalf of the reader of this publication.

The scanning, uploading and distribution of this publication via the Internet or via any other means without the permission of the publisher is illegal and punishable by law. Please purchase only authorized editions and do not participate in or encourage piracy of copyrightable materials.

ISBN 13 TP: 978-1-64095-622-3

ISBN 13 eBook: 978-1-64095-623-0

For Worldwide Distribution, Printed in the U.S.A.

1 2025

Ahead of you stretches your future like a road leading into the distance. Along that road are ambitions you wish to accomplish...desires you wish to gratify.

To bring your ambitions and desires to fulfillment, you must be successful with money. Use the financial principles made clear in the pages which follow. Let them guide you away from the stringencies of a lean wallet to that fuller, happier life a full wallet makes possible.

Like the law of gravity, they are universal and unchanging. May they prove for you, as they have proven to so many others, a sure key to a fat wallet, larger bank balances and gratifying financial progress.

CONTENTS

	Foreword............................... 9
	Preface 11
Day 1	Babylon, the Place 13
Day 2	Who Wants Gold........................19
Day 3	The Richest Man 25
Day 4	Wealth Grows From a Tiny Seed 31
Day 5	A Desire to Prosper..................... 37
Day 6	Seven Cures...for a Thin Wallet........... 43
Day 7	Fatten Your Wallet 49
Day 8	Curb Your Appetite..................... 53
Day 9	Multiply Your Gold.....................57
Day 10	Guard Your Treasures 61
Day 11	Your Home, Your Investment............. 65
Day 12	Future Income......................... 69
Day 13	Earn More............................ 73
Day 14	Good Blessings or Good Luck 79
Day 15	Chances of Profit 83

Day 16	Loss and Later Regret	87
Day 17	The Poor Procrastinator	93
Day 18	Profit Robber	99
Day 19	Five Laws of Gold	103
Day 20	Beware	107
Day 21	The Gold Lender	111
Day 22	Borrowing and Lending	115
Day 23	Human-Effort Loans	121
Day 24	Hopeless Debt	127
Day 25	Secrets of the Token Chest	131
Day 26	Babylon's Walls	137
Day 27	Fully Protected	143
Day 28	A Different Color of Life	147
Day 29	The Tale	153
Day 30	A Free Soul	159
	About the Author	169

FOREWORD

The Richest Man in Babylon in Ten Minutes a Day gives you a valuable set of key financial-success principles told via a quirky ancient story. In these brief but beefy 10-minute bursts of rich wisdom, you can master the success system that has made many people wealthy—not only financially, but in developing long-term personal happiness, peace of mind, and harmonious relationships.

The Richest Man in Babylon, first published in 1926 by George S. Clason, is a personal finance book that continues to be read worldwide for its wisdom. Clason shares his financial advice with readers through a series of fictional parables set in the ancient Mesopotamian city of Babylon. The story's characters face obstacles to wealth and success, including low wages, poor spending habits, indebtedness, and even enslavement—but they overcome each challenge through hard work, discipline, and a structured system of saving and spending.

The Richest Man in Babylon has had a profound impact on the field of personal finance, influencing many of today's most renowned financial experts. His core teachings—including pay yourself first, live within your means, and invest in what you know—remain extremely relevant in today's economic environments.

The Richest Man in Babylon's enduring popularity is proven by its perpetual publication a century later, with more than two million copies sold, so far.

The story revolves around Arkad, a poor scribe who becomes the wealthiest man in Babylon through his financial acumen and discipline. Throughout the narrative, readers encounter various characters facing financial challenges similar to those we face today. These characters learn valuable lessons about debt management, building passive income, and making sound investment decisions. Applying the principles leads to financial success.

The Richest Man in Babylon is considered a definitive source on financial advice—and we believe you will agree!

The book is divided into 30 segments, easily read in 10 minutes and absorbed for a lifetime of benefit. Of course you have any number of reading options—one a day, a cluster of a few a day, or read the entire book in an evening. No matter your reading schedule preference, you will discover every page is filled with the best of what *The Richest Man in Babylon* has to share with you.

Sound Wisdom Publishing

PREFACE

by George S. Clason
Author of the Original
The Richest Man in Babylon

Our prosperity as a nation depends upon the personal financial prosperity of each of us as individuals.

This book deals with the personal successes of each of us. Success means accomplishments as the result of our own efforts and abilities. Proper preparation is the key to our success. Our acts can be no wiser than our thoughts. Our thinking can be no wiser than our understanding.

This book of cures for lean wallets has been termed a guide to financial understanding. That, indeed, is its purpose: to offer those who are ambitious for financial success an insight which will aid them to acquire money, to keep money and to make their surpluses earn more money.

In the pages which follow, we are taken back to Babylon, the cradle in which was nurtured the basic principles of finance now recognized and used the world over.

To new readers the author is happy to extend the wish that its pages may contain for them the same inspiration for growing bank accounts, greater financial successes and the solution of difficult personal financial problems so enthusiastically reported by readers from coast to coast.

To the business executives who have distributed these tales in such generous quantities to friends, relatives, employees and associates, the author takes this opportunity to express his gratitude. No endorsement could be higher than that of practical men who appreciate its teachings because they, themselves, have worked up to important successes by applying the very principles it advocates.

Babylon became the wealthiest city of the ancient world because its citizens were the richest people of their time. They appreciated the value of money. They practiced sound financial principles in acquiring money, keeping money and making their money earn more money. They provided for themselves what we all desire…incomes for the future.

G. S. C.

Day 1

BABYLON, THE PLACE

In the pages of history there lives no city more glamorous than Babylon. Its very name conjures visions of wealth and splendor. Its treasures of gold and jewels were fabulous. One naturally pictures such a wealthy city as located in a suitable setting of tropical luxury, surrounded by rich natural resources of forests, and mines.

Such was not the case. It was located beside the Euphrates River, in a flat, arid valley. It had no forests, no mines—not even stone for building. It was not even located upon a natural trade-route. The rainfall was insufficient to raise crops.

Babylon is an outstanding example of man's ability to achieve great objectives, using whatever means are at his disposal. All of the resources supporting this large city were man-developed. All of its riches were man-made.

Babylon possessed just two natural resources—a fertile soil and water in the river. With one of the greatest engineering accomplishments of this or any other day, Babylonian engineers diverted the waters from the river by means of dams and immense irrigation canals. Far out across that arid valley went these canals to pour the life giving waters over the fertile soil. This ranks among the first engineering feats known to history. Such abundant crops as were the reward of this irrigation system the world had never seen.

Fortunately, during its long existence, Babylon was ruled by successive lines of kings to whom conquest and plunder were but incidental. While it engaged in many wars, most of these were local or defensive against ambitious conquerors from other countries who coveted the fabulous treasures of Babylon. *The outstanding rulers of Babylon live in history because of their wisdom, enterprise and justice. Babylon produced no strutting monarchs who sought to conquer the known world that all nations might pay homage to their egotism.*

As a city, Babylon exists no more. When those energizing human forces that built and maintained the city for thousands of years were withdrawn, it soon became a deserted ruin.

Today, this valley of the Euphrates, once a populous irrigated farming district, is again a wind-swept arid waste. Scant grass and desert shrubs strive for existence against the windblown sands. Gone are the fertile fields, the mammoth cities and the long caravans of rich merchandise.

We have proved that 8,000 years ago, the Sumerites, who inhabited Babylonia, were living in walled cities. Their inhabitants were not mere barbarians living within protecting walls. *They were an educated and enlightened people. So far as written history goes, they were the first engineers, the first astronomers, the first mathematicians, the first financiers and the first people to have a written language.*

In addition to irrigating the valley lands, Babylonian engineers completed another project of similar magnitude. By means of an elaborate drainage system they reclaimed an immense area of swamp land at the mouths of the Euphrates and Tigris Rivers and put this also under cultivation, resulting in the remarkable fertility of the soil and the bountiful harvest of wheat and barley.

Against the walls of Babylon marched, in turn, the victorious armies of almost every conqueror of that age of wars of conquest. A host of kings laid siege to Babylon, but always in vain. The city of Babylon was organized much like a modern city. There were streets and shops. Peddlers offered their wares through residential districts. Priests officiated in magnificent temples. *The Babylonians were skilled in the arts. These included sculpture, painting, weaving, gold working and the manufacture of metal weapons and agricultural implements.*

At a very early period when the rest of the world was still hacking at trees with stone-headed axes, or hunting and fighting with flint-pointed spears and arrows, the

Babylonians were using axes, spears and arrows with metal heads. *The Babylonians were clever financiers and traders. So far as we know, they were the original inventors of money as a means of exchange, of promissory notes and written titles to property.*

One of the outstanding wonders of Babylon was the immense walls surrounding the city. It is estimated the later walls were about 160 feet high, the total length between 9 and 11 miles. Babylon was never entered by hostile armies until about 540 years before the birth of Christ.

Cyrus, one of the great conquerors of that period, intended to attack the city and hoped to take its impregnable walls. Cyrus, thereupon, entered the open gates and took possession without resistance. Advisors of the King of Babylon, persuaded him to go forth to meet Cyrus and give him battle without waiting for the city to be besieged. In the succeeding defeat to the Babylonian army, it fled away from the city. Cyrus, thereupon, entered the open gates and took possession without resistance.

Thereafter the power and prestige of the city gradually waned until, in the course of a few hundred years, it was eventually abandoned, deserted, left for the winds and storms to level once again to that desert earth from which its grandeur had originally been built. Babylon had fallen, never to rise again, but to it civilization owes much.

The eons of time have crumbled to dust the proud walls of its temples, *but the wisdom of Babylon endures.*

Richest Ruminations

Motivation and mutual benefit are keys to success—when the rulers and the people were unified in using their skills and talents to benefit the whole of their city, amazing advancements were accomplished. When the leadership dynamics changed and unscrupulous outside influences came into play, destruction was not far behind.

How high are the walls you have built? Do they protect your values, morals, and ethics? What applies to countries, states, cities, and neighborhoods also applies to individual rise and falls. Best to routinely take inventory of who you allow to influence you—as well as assess your personal motives and intentions to prevent a disaster that may affect your career, finances, family, all you hold dear.

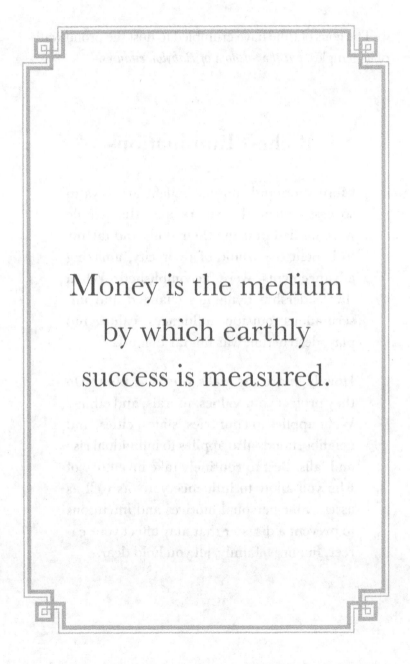

Money is the medium by which earthly success is measured.

Day 2

WHO WANTS GOLD

Bansir, the chariot builder of Babylon, was thoroughly discouraged. From his seat upon the low wall surrounding his property, he gazed sadly at his simple home and the open workshop in which stood a partially completed chariot.

His wife frequently appeared at the open door. Her furtive glances in his direction reminded him that the meal bag was almost empty and he should be at work finishing the chariot so he could collect from his wealthy customer.

Nevertheless, his fat, muscular body sat stolidly upon the wall. His slow mind was struggling patiently with a problem for which he could find no answer. Bansir was too engrossed in his own problem to hear or heed the confused hubbub of the busy city. It was the unexpected twanging of the strings from a familiar lyre that aroused him from his reverie. He turned to see his sensitive, smiling face of his best friend—Kobbi, the musician. "I rejoice with thee in thy good fortune. Pray, from thy wallet which must be bulging else thou wouldst be busy in your shop, extract but two humble shekels and lend them to me until after the noblemen's feast this night. Thou wilt not miss them ere they are returned."

"If I did have two shekels," Bansir responded gloomily, "to no one could I lend them—not even to you, my best of friends; for they would be my fortune—my entire fortune. No one lends his entire fortune, not even to his best friend."

"What," exclaimed Kobbi with genuine surprise. "Thou hast not one shekel in your wallet, yet sit like a statue upon a wall! Why not complete that chariot? How else canst thou provide for thy noble appetite? Tis not like thee. Where is thy endless energy? Doth something distress thee?"

"A torment it is," Bansir agreed. "It began with a dream, a senseless dream, in which I thought I was a man of means. From my belt hung a handsome wallet, heavy with coins. There were shekels which I cast with careless freedom to the beggars; there were pieces of silver with which I did buy finery for my wife; there were pieces of gold which made me feel assured of the future. A glorious feeling of contentment was within me! You would not have known me for thy hardworking friend."

"A pleasant dream, indeed," commented Kobbi, "but why should such pleasant feelings as it aroused turn thee into a glum statue upon the wall?"

"Why, indeed!" said Bansir. "Because when I awoke and remembered how empty was my wallet, a feeling of rebellion swept over me. After half a lifetime of hard labor, I admit that my wallet is as empty as thine."

"Never, in all the years of our friendship, didst thou talk like this before, Bansir." Kobbi was puzzled.

"Never in all those years did I think like this before. From early dawn until darkness stopped me, I have labored to build the finest chariots any man could make, soft-heartedly hoping someday my worthy deeds would bring me great prosperity. Why cannot we have our just share of the good things? Perhaps there is some secret we might learn if we but sought from those who knew," replied Bansir thoughtfully.

"This very day," suggested Kobbi, "I did pass our old friend, Arkad, riding in his golden chariot."

"He is so rich, I fear if I should meet him in the darkness of the night, I should lay my hands upon his fat wallet," said Bansir.

"Nonsense," reproved Kobbi, *"a man's wealth is not in the wallet he carries. A fat wallet quickly empties if there be no golden stream to refill it.* Arkad has an income that constantly keeps his wallet full, no matter how liberally he spends."

Bansir said, "I wish an income that will keep flowing into my wallet whether I sit upon the wall or travel to far lands. Arkad must know how a man can make an income for himself. Dost suppose it is something he could make clear to a mind as slow as mine?"

"Me thinks he did teach his knowledge to his son, Nomasir," Kobbi responded. "Did he not go to Nineveh and, so it is told at the inn, become, without aid from his father, one of the richest men in that city?"

"Kobbi, it costs nothing to ask wise advice from a good friend and Arkad was always that. We are weary of being without gold in the midst of plenty. We wish to become men of means. Come, let us go to Arkad and ask how we, also, may acquire incomes for ourselves."

"Thou makest me to realize the reason why we have never found any measure of wealth. We never sought it. In those things toward which we exerted our best endeavors we succeeded. With a new understanding we shall find honourable ways to accomplish our desires. Let us go to Arkad this very day," Bansir urged.

Richest Ruminations

Have you and a friend or spouse had similar conversations about your lot in life? Like Bansir, are you discouraged, realizing that you've worked so long and so hard yet you're still living "chariot-to-chariot," paycheck to paycheck?

"Thou makest me to realize the reason why we have never found any measure of wealth. We never sought it." How did Kobbi's statement resonate with you?

Have you labored to build your career, business, or move up the ladder at work? Has your purpose been devoted to delivering your best endeavors? Have you succeeded? Are you excited to learn more so you can prosper more—to gain a new understanding of honorable ways to accomplish your desires?

Seeking wisdom from those who have already acquired wealth is the best lesson learned.

Day 3

THE RICHEST MAN

In old Babylon there once lived a certain very rich man named Arkad. Far and wide he was famed for his great wealth. Also was he famed for being generous to his charities and his family. He was liberal in his own expenses. But nevertheless each year his wealth increased more rapidly than he spent it.

And there were certain friends of younger days who came to him and said: "You, Arkad, are more fortunate than we. You have become the richest man in all Babylon while we struggle for existence. Yet, once we were equal. Neither the studies nor the games did you outshine us. And in the years since, you have been no more an honorable citizen than we. Nor have you worked harder or more faithfully. Why should a fickle fate single you out to enjoy all the good things of life and ignore us who are equally deserving?"

Thereupon Arkad remonstrated with them, saying, "If you have not acquired more than a bare existence in the years since we were youths, it is because *you either have failed to learn the laws that govern the building of wealth, or else you do not observe them.*

"Fickle Fate brings no permanent good to anyone. On the contrary, ruin comes to almost everyone showered with unearned gold. Wanton spenders soon dissipate all they receive and are left with overwhelming appetites and desires with no ability to gratify. Yet others become misers and hoard their wealth, fearing to spend. They live in fear of robbers and doom."

His friends admitted his words were true, and they asked him to explain. So Arkad continued: "In my youth I saw all the good things to bring happiness and contentment. And I realized that wealth increased the potency. *Wealth is a power. With wealth many things are possible.*

"And, when I realized all this, I decided to myself that I would claim my share of the good things of life. I would not be one of those who stand afar off, enviously watching others enjoy. On the contrary, I would make myself a guest at this banquet of good things.

"Being, as you know, the son of a humble merchant, one of a large family with no hope of an inheritance, and not being endowed, as you have so frankly said, with superior powers or wisdom, I decided that *if I was to achieve what I desired, time and study would be required.*

"As for time, all people have it in abundance. Each of you have let slip by sufficient time to have made yourselves wealthy. You admit you have nothing to show except your good families, of which you can be justly proud. Our wise teacher taught us learning was of two kinds: one being what we learned and knew, and two to find out what we did not know. I decided to find out how to accumulate wealth, and make this my task and do it well. I found employment as a scribe in the hall of records. I labored for months, yet had naught to show. My determination was strong.

"One day Algamish, the money lender, came to the house of the city master and ordered a copy of the Ninth Law, and he said to me, 'I must have this in two days, and if the task is done by that time, two coppers will I give to thee.'

"So I labored hard, but the law was long, and when Algamish returned the task was unfinished. He was angry. So I said to him, 'Algamish, you are a very rich man. Tell me how I may also become rich, and I will carve upon the clay all night; when the sun rises it shall be completed.'

"He smiled at me and replied, 'You are a forward knave, but we will call it a bargain.'

"All that night I carved, and when he returned at sunup, the tablets were complete. 'Now,' I said, 'tell me what you promised.'

"'You have fulfilled your part of our bargain, my son,' he said to me kindly, 'and I am ready to fulfill mine. Mark you well my words, for if you do not you will fail to grasp the truth that I will tell you, and you will think that your night's work has been in vain.'

"Then he looked at me shrewdly from under his shaggy brows and said in a low, forceful tone,

'I found the road to wealth when I decided that a part of all I earned was mine to keep.'

"'Is that all you have to tell me?' I asked. 'But all I earn is mine to keep, is it not?' I demanded.

"'Far from it,' he replied. 'Do you not pay the garment and shoe maker? Do you not pay for the things you eat? Can you live in Babylon without spending? What have you to show for your earnings of the past month? The past year? Fool! *You pay to everyone but yourself.* You might as well be a slave and work for what your master gives you to eat and wear. If you did keep for yourself one-tenth of all you earn, how much would you have in ten years?'

"I answered, 'As much as I earn in one year.'

"You speak but half the truth,' he retorted. 'Every gold piece you save is a slave to work for you. Every copper it earns is its child that also can earn for you. *To become wealthy, what you save must earn,* and its children must earn, that all may help to give you the abundance you crave. You think I cheat you for your long night's work, but I am paying you a thousand times over if you have the intelligence to grasp the truth I offer you.'"

Richest Ruminations

Do you have childhood or even college friends who have successfully succeeded in their chosen field way beyond where you are in life at this time? Have you ever considered asking their advice about how you too can advance toward a more financially abundant and stable lifestyle?

What do you think about the "truth" offered by Algamish to Arkad? Do you believe this seemingly "simple" advice is worth exploring? Are you a saver and investor? Will you take this advice seriously—to pay yourself first and have that savings earn you more?

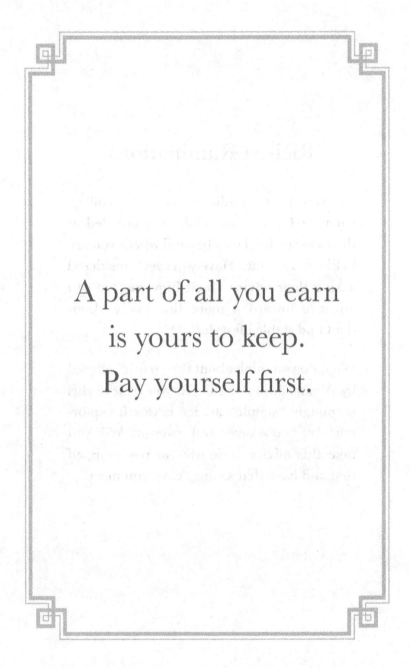

A part of all you earn is yours to keep.
Pay yourself first.

Day 4

WEALTH GROWS FROM A TINY SEED

Algamish continued, "'Wealth, like a tree, grows from a tiny seed. The first copper you save is the seed from which your tree of wealth shall grow. The sooner you plant that seed the sooner shall the tree grow. And the more faithfully you nourish and water that tree with consistent savings, the sooner may you bask in contentment beneath its shade.'

"So saying, he went away. I thought much about what he had said to me, and it seemed reasonable. So I decided to try it. Each time I was paid *I took one from each ten pieces of copper and hid it away.* And strange as it may seem, I was no shorter of funds, than before. *I noticed little difference as I managed to get along without it.* But often I was tempted, as my hoard began to grow, to spend it for some of the good things the merchants displayed. But I wisely refrained.

"After the twelfth month, Algamish returned and asked, 'Son, have you paid to yourself not less than one-tenth of all you have earned for the past year?'

"I answered proudly, 'Yes, master, I have.' 'That is good, and what have you done with it?'

"I gave it to Azmur, the brick maker, who was traveling over the far seas, and would buy for me rare jewels. When he returns we shall sell these at high prices and divide the earnings."

"'Every fool must learn,' he growled, 'why trust the knowledge of a brick maker about jewels? Would you go to the bread maker to inquire about the stars? No, you would go to the astrologer, if you had power to think. Your savings are gone, youth, you have jerked your wealth-tree up by the roots. But plant another. Try again. Next time ask advice about jewels from a jewel merchant. And about sheep, go to the herdsman. *Advice is freely given away, but watch that you take only what is worth having.* He who takes advice about his savings from one who is inexperienced in such matters, shall pay with his savings for proving the falsity of their opinions.' Saying this, he went away.

"And it was as he said. For the Phoenicians are scoundrels and sold to Azmur worthless bits of glass that looked like gems. But as Algamish had advised me, *I again saved each tenth copper, for I now had formed the habit and it was no longer difficult.*

"Again, twelve months later, Algamish came to the room of the scribes and asked, "What progress have you made since last I saw you?"

"I have paid myself faithfully and entrusted my savings to Agger the shield maker to buy bronze, and each fourth month he does pay me the rental."

"'That is good. And what do you do with the rental?'

"I have a great feast with honey and fine wine and spiced cake. Also I have bought a scarlet tunic. And some day I shall buy me a young ass upon which to ride."

To which Algamish laughed, "You do eat the children of your savings. Then how do you expect them to work for you? And how can they have children that will also work for you? First get thee an army of golden slaves and then many a rich banquet may you enjoy without regret." So saying he again went away.

"Nor did I again see him for two years, when he once more returned and his face was full of deep lines and his eyes drooped, for he was becoming a very old man. And he said to me, "Arkad, hast thou yet achieved the wealth thou dreamed of?"

And I answered, "Not yet all that I desire, but some I have and it earns more, and its earnings earn more."

"And do you still take the advice of brick makers?"

"About brick making they give good advice," I retorted.

"'Arkad,' he continued, 'you have learned your lessons well. You first learned to live upon less than you could earn. Next you learned to seek advice from those who were competent through their own experiences to give it. And, lastly, you have learned to make gold work for you.'

"'You have taught yourself how to acquire money, how to keep it, and how to use it. Therefore, you are competent for a responsible position. I am becoming an old man. My sons think only of spending and give no thought to earning. My interests are great and I fear too much for me to look after. If you will go to Nippur and look after my lands there, I shall make you my partner and you shall share in my estate.'"

Richest Ruminations

How easy—or hard—would it be for you to consistently save 10 percent of everything you receive? How long do you think it would take for that habit to form, knowing it will lead to wealth.

Do you understand that the "children" talked about are actually earnings upon earnings that you can generate for wealth with first paying yourself and then investing that 10 percent to reap more to invest more? Can you alter your mindset to make this a reality?

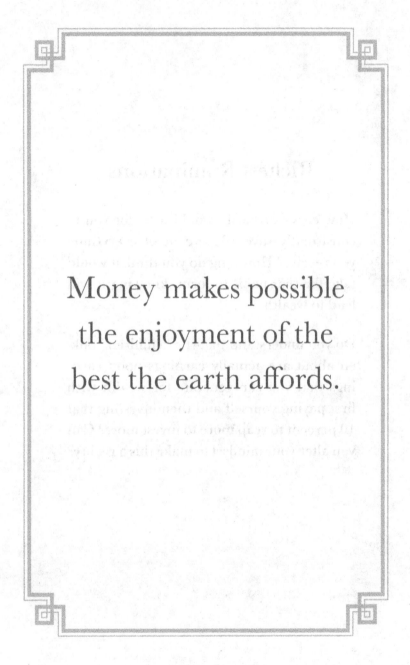

Money makes possible the enjoyment of the best the earth affords.

Day 5

A DESIRE TO PROSPER

Arkad continued with his story, "So I went to Nippur and took charge of Algamish's holdings, which were large. And because I was full of ambition and because I had mastered the three laws of successfully handling wealth, I increased greatly the value of his properties. I prospered much. When the spirit of Algamish departed, I shared in his estate as he had arranged under the law."

When Arkad had finished his tale, one of his two friends who came for advice said, "You were indeed fortunate that Algamish made you an heir."

Arkad said, "Fortunate only in that I had the desire to prosper before I first met him. For four years I proved my definiteness of purpose by keeping one-tenth of all earned. Would you call a fisherman lucky who for years studied the habits of the fish that with each changing wind he could cast his nets and catch them? *Opportunity wastes no time with those who are unprepared.*"

"You had strong will power to keep on after you lost your first year's savings. You are unusual in that way," spoke up the other friend.

"Will power!?" retorted Arkad. "What nonsense. Do you think will power gives a man the strength to lift a burden the camel cannot carry, or to draw a load the oxen cannot budge? *Will power is but the unflinching purpose to carry a task you set for yourself to fulfillment.* If I set for myself a task, be it ever so trifling, I shall see it through. How else shall I have confidence in myself to do important things? When I set a task for myself, I complete it. Therefore, I am careful not to start difficult and impractical tasks, because I love leisure."

The other friend spoke up, "If what you tell is true, and it does seem as you have said, reasonable, then being so simple, if all did it, there would not be enough wealth to go around."

"*Wealth grows wherever men exert energy,*" Arkad replied. "If a rich man builds him a new palace, is the gold he pays out gone? No, the brickmaker has part of it and the laborer has part of it, and the artist has part of it. And everyone who labors upon the house has part of it. Yet when the palace is completed, is it not worth all it cost? And is the ground upon which it stands not worth more because it is there? And is the ground that adjoins it not worth more because it is there? Wealth grows in mysterious ways. No one can prophesy the limit of it. Have not the Phoenicians built great cities on barren coasts with the wealth that comes from their ships of commerce on the seas?"

"What then do you advise us to do that we also may become rich?" asked his friends. "The years have passed and we are no longer young men and we have nothing put back."

"I advise that you take the wisdom of Algamish and say to yourselves, *'A part of all I earn is mine to keep.'* Say it in the morning when you first arise. Say it at noon. Say it at night. Say it each hour of every day. Say it to yourself until the words stand out like letters of fire in the sky.

"Fill yourself with the thought.

"Take out whatever portion seems wise, but no less than one-tenth and lay it aside. Soon you will realize what a rich feeling it is to own your own treasure. As it grows it will stimulate you. A new joy of life will thrill you. Then learn to *make your treasure work for you.* Make it your slave. Make its children and its children's children work for you.

"Insure an income for your future with greatest caution that it be not lost. Usurious rates of return are deceitful sirens that sing to lure the unwary upon the rocks of loss and remorse. Provide also that thy family may not want when you're gone to another realm. For such protection it is always possible to make provision with small payments at regular intervals. Therefore delays not in expectation of a large sum becoming available for such a wise purpose.

"Counsel with wise men. Seek the advice of those whose daily work is handling money. Let them save you from such an error as I myself made in entrusting my money to the judgment of Azmur, the brickmaker. A small return and a safe one is far more desirable than risk.

"Enjoy life while you are here. Do not overstrain or try to save too much. If one-tenth of all you earn is as much as you can comfortably keep, be content to keep this portion. Live otherwise according to your income and let not yourself get miserly, afraid to spend. Life is good and life is rich with things worthwhile and things to enjoy."

The two friends and others who had joined them thanked Arkad and went away. Some were silent because they had no imagination and could not understand. Some were sarcastic because they thought that one so rich should divide with old friends not so fortunate. But some had in their eyes a new light. They realized that Algamish had come back each time to the room of the scribes because *he was watching a man work his way out of darkness into light.* When that man had found the light, a place awaited him.

No one could fill that place until he had for himself worked out his own understanding, until he was ready for opportunity. These latter were the ones, who, in the following years, frequently revisited Arkad, who received them gladly. He counseled with them and gave them freely of his wisdom as those of broad experience are always glad to do. And he assisted them in investing their savings that it would bring in a good interest with safety and would neither be lost nor entangled in investments that paid no dividends.

The turning point in the chariot-maker and the musician's lives came on the day when they realized the truth that had come from Algamish to Arkad and from Arkad to them.

Richest Ruminations

Are you prepared for opportunities coming your way to increase your wealth? Have you been working diligently in your current position so that those watching see your steadfastness and sincere dedication to learn what they have to teach?

Do you exert every effort to see each task through to the end—or are you prone to think things will work out no matter the effort? Are you committed to working your way out of the darkness into the light of a better, richer life?

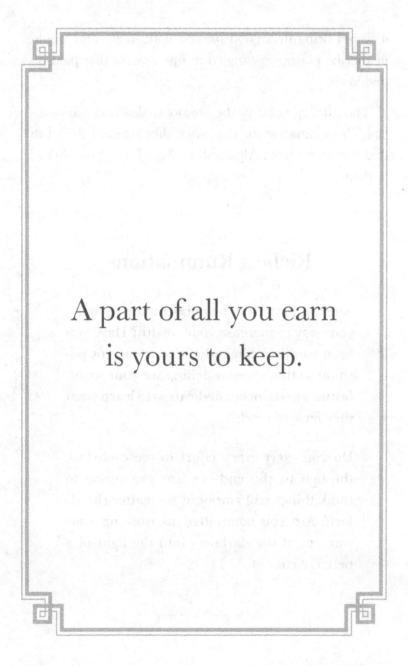

A part of all you earn
is yours to keep.

Day 6

SEVEN CURES...FOR A THIN WALLET

The glory of Babylon endures. Down through the ages its reputation comes to us as the richest of cities, its treasures as fabulous. Yet it was not always so. The riches of Babylon were the results of the wisdom of its people.

They first had to learn how to become wealthy. When the Good King, Sargon, returned to Babylon after defeating his enemies, he was confronted with a serious situation: "The laborers are without employment. The merchants have few customers. The farmers are unable to sell their produce. The people have not enough gold to buy food."

"But where has all the gold gone that we spent for our city's great improvements?" demanded the King.

"It has found its way," responded the Chancellor, "into the possession of a few very rich men of our city. It filtered through the fingers of most our people. Now that the stream of gold has ceased to flow, most of our people have nothing to show for their earnings."

The King was thoughtful for some time, then asked, "Why should so few be able to acquire all the gold? Why should not all the people learn how to accumulate gold and therefore become themselves rich and prosperous? Who knows best in all our city how to become wealthy, Chancellor? Who has amassed the greatest wealth, in Babylon?"

"It is Arkad. He is richest man in Babylon. Bring him before me on the morrow." The following day, as the King had decreed, Arkad appeared before him, straight and sprightly despite his three score years and ten.

"Arkad," spoke the King, "is it true thou art the richest man in Babylon? *How have you become so wealthy?*"

"By taking advantage of opportunities available to all citizens of our good city."

"Thou hadst nothing to start with?"

"Only a great desire for wealth. Besides this, nothing."

"Arkad," continued the King, "our city is in a very unhappy state because only a few men know how to acquire wealth and therefore monopolize it, while the mass of our citizens lack the knowledge of how to keep any part of the gold they receive. It is my desire that Babylon be the wealthiest city in the world. Therefore, it must be a city of many wealthy people. Therefore, we must teach them how to acquire riches. Tell me, Arkad, is there any secret to acquiring wealth? Can it be taught?"

"It is practical, your majesty. *What one man knows can be taught to others.*" The king's eyes glowed. "Arkad, thou speaketh the words I wish to hear. Wilt thou lend thyself to this great cause? Wilt thou teach thy knowledge to a school for teachers, each of whom shall teach others until there are enough trained to teach these truths to every worthy subject in my domain?"

Arkad bowed and said, "I am thy humble servant to command. Whatever knowledge I possess will I gladly give for the betterment of my fellowmen and the glory of my King. Let your good chancellor arrange for me a class of one hundred men and *I will teach to them those seven cures which did fatten my wallet,* than which there was none leaner in all Babylon."

A fortnight later, in compliance with the King's command, the chosen hundred assembled in the great hall of the Temple of Learning, seated upon colorful rings in a semicircle. Arkad sat beside a small taboret upon which smoked a sacred lamp sending forth a strange and pleasing odor.

"Behold the richest man in Babylon," whispered a student, nudging his neighbor as Arkad arose. "He is but a man even as the rest of us."

"As a dutiful subject of our great King," Arkad began, "I stand before you in his service. Because once I was a poor youth who did greatly desire gold, and because I found knowledge that enabled me to acquire it, he asks that I impart unto you my knowledge. I started my fortune in the humblest way. I had no advantage not enjoyed as fully by you and every citizen in Babylon.

"I loathed my lean wallet and its useless emptiness. I desired it be round and full, clinking with the sound of gold. Therefore, I sought every remedy and I found seven. I will explain the seven cures for a lean wallet which I recommend to all men who desire much gold. Each day for seven days will I explain to you one of the seven remedies.

"Listen attentively to the knowledge that I impart. Debate it with me. Discuss it among yourselves. *Learn these lessons thoroughly, that ye may also plant in your own wallet the seed of wealth.* First must each of you start wisely to build a fortune of his own. Then wilt thou be competent, and only then, to teach these truths to others.

"I shall teach to you in simple ways how to fatten your wallets. This is the first step leading to the temple of wealth, and no man may climb who cannot plant his feet firmly upon the first step.

"We shall now consider the first cure."

Richest Ruminations

Do you live in a wealthy country? State? Community? If yes, great! If not, do you see opportunities to increase the wealth around you?

Are the leaders in your region or city committed to improving the living standards, offering opportunities for people to improve their lot in life?

Money is plentiful for those who understand the simple laws which govern its acquisition.

Day 7

FATTEN YOUR WALLET

Arkad addressed a thoughtful man in the second row. "My good friend, at what craft do you work?"

"I," replied the man, "am a scribe and carve records upon the clay tablets."

"Even at such labor did I myself earn my first coppers. Therefore, thou hast the same opportunity to build a fortune." He spoke to a florid-faced man, farther back. "Pray tell also what you do to earn thy bread?"

"I," responded this man, "am a meat butcher. I buy goats the farmers raise and kill them and sell the meat to the housewives and the hides to the sandal makers."

"Because you also labor and earn, thou hast every advantage to succeed that I did possess."

In this way Arkad proceeded to find out how each man labored to earn his living. After he had questioned them, he said, "Now, my students, you can see that there are many trades and labors at which men may earn coins. Each of the ways of earning is a stream of gold from which the worker can divert by his labors a portion to his own wallet. Therefore into the wallet of each of you flows a stream of coins large or small according to his ability. Is it not so?"

They agreed that it was so. "Then," continued Arkad, "if each of you desires to build for himself a fortune, is it not wise to start by utilizing that source of wealth you have already established?"

To this they agreed. Then Arkad turned to a humble man who had declared himself an egg merchant. "If you select one of your baskets and put into it each morning ten eggs and take out from it each evening nine eggs, what will eventually happen?"

"In time it will become overflowing."

"Why?"

"Because each day I put in one more egg than I take out."

Arkad turned to the class with a smile. "Does any man here have a lean wallet?"

First they looked amused. Then they laughed. Lastly they waved their wallets in jest. "All right," he continued, "Now I shall tell you the first remedy I learned to cure a lean wallet. Do exactly as I have suggested to the egg merchant. *For every ten coins you place within your wallet, take out for use only nine.* Your wallet will start to fatten at once and its increasing weight *will feel good in your hand and bring satisfaction to thy soul.*

"Scoff not what I say because of its simplicity. Truth is always simple. I told you I would tell you how I built my fortune. This was my beginning. I, too, carried a lean wallet and cursed it because there was nothing within to satisfy my desires. But when I began to take out from my wallet only nine parts of ten I put in, it began to fatten. So will yours.

"Now I will tell a strange truth, the reason for which I know not. When I ceased to pay out more than nine-tenths of my earnings, I managed to get along just as well. I was not shorter than before. Also, before long, coins came to me more easily than before. Surely it is a law that unto him who keep and spend not a certain part of all his earnings, shall gold come more easily. Likewise, him whose wallet is empty does gold avoid.

"Which do you desire the most? Is it the gratification of thy desires of each day, a jewel, a bit of finery, better raiment, more food; things quickly gone and forgotten? Or is it substantial belongings, gold, lands, herds, merchandise,

51

income-bringing investments? The coins you take from your wallet bring the first. The coins you leave within your wallet will bring the latter.

"This, my students, was the **first cure** I discovered for my lean wallet: *'For each ten coins I put in, spend only nine.'* Debate this amongst yourselves. If anyone proves it untrue, tell me upon the morrow when we shall meet again."

Richest Ruminations

Into your wallet flows a stream of money, large or small according to your ability. So if you desire to build a fortune, is it not wise to start using that source of wealth you have already established?

The first cure to fatten your wallet is to save one of every ten dollars you bring home. Is this a reasonable sacrifice for you to make, knowing in the long run you are establishing a habit that will reap great rewards?

Day 8

CURB YOUR APPETITE

Some of your members, my students, have asked me this: How can a man keep one-tenth of all he earns in his wallet when all the coins he earns are not enough for his necessary expenses?"

So did Arkad address his students upon the second day.

"Yesterday how many of you carried lean wallets?"

"All of us," answered the class.

"Yet, you do not all earn the same. Some earn much more than others. Some have much larger families to support. Yet, all wallets were equally lean. Now I will tell you an unusual truth about men and sons of men. It is this: *What each of us calls our 'necessary expenses' will always grow to equal our incomes unless we protest to the contrary.*

"Confuse not the necessary expenses with your desires. Each of you, together with your good families, have more desires than your earnings can gratify. Therefore, are your earnings spent to gratify these desires insofar as they will go. Still you have many ungratified desires.

"All men are burdened with more desires than they can gratify. Because of my wealth do you think I may gratify every desire? This a false idea. There are limits to my time. There are limits to my strength. There are limits to the distance I may travel. There are limits to what I may eat. There are limits to the zest with which I may enjoy.

"I say to you that just as weeds grow in a field wherever the farmer leaves space for their roots, even so freely do desires grow in men whenever there is a possibility of their being gratified. Your desires are a multitude and those you may gratify are but few.

"Study thoughtfully your accustomed habits of living. Herein may be most often found certain accepted expenses that may wisely be reduced or eliminated. Let thy motto be *one hundred percent of appreciated value demanded for each coin spent.*

"Therefore, record each thing for which you desire to spend. Select those that are necessary and others that are possible through the expenditure of nine-tenths of your income. Cross out the rest and consider them but a part of that great multitude of desires that must go unsatisfied and regret them not.

"*Budget your necessary expenses.* Touch not the one-tenth that is fattening thy wallet. Let this be your great desire that is being fulfilled. Keep working with your budget, keep adjusting it to help thee. Make it thy first assistant in defending thy fattening wallet."

Hereupon one of the students, wearing a robe of red and gold, arose and said, "I am a free man.

I believe that it is my right to enjoy the good things of life. Therefore do I rebel against the slavery of a budget which determines just how much I may spend and for what. I feel it would take much pleasure from my life and make me little more than a pack-ass to carry a burden."

To him Arkad replied, "Who, my friend, would determine your budget?"

"I would make it for myself," responded the protesting one.

"In that case were a pack-ass to budget his burden would he include therein jewels and rugs and heavy bars of gold? Not so. He would include hay and grain and a bag of water for the desert trail.

"The purpose of a budget is to help your wallet to fatten. It is to assist thee to have necessities and, insofar as attainable, your other desires. It is to enable you to realize your most cherished desires by defending them from casual wishes. Like a bright light in a dark cave *your budget shows up the leaks from your wallet and enables you to stop them and control your expenditures for definite and gratifying purposes.*

"This, then, is the **second cure** for a lean wallet: budget your expenses that you may have coins to pay for your necessities, to pay for your enjoyments and to gratify your worthwhile desires without spending more than nine-tenths of your earnings."

Richest Ruminations

Do you struggle paying your necessary expenses yet give in to what you know are desires rather than necessities? Do you confuse your necessary expenses with your desires?

How would keeping a record of all that you spend help curb your appetite for desires and put you on track to fatten your wallet?

Day 9

MULTIPLY YOUR GOLD

Behold your lean wallet is fattening. You have disciplined yourself to leave there one-tenth of all you earn. You have controlled your expenditures to protect your growing treasure. Next, we will consider means to put your treasure to labor and to increase. Gold in a wallet is gratifying to own and satisfies a miserly soul—but earns nothing. The gold we may retain from our earnings is but the start. The earnings it will make shall build our fortunes." So spoke Arkad upon the third day to his class.

"How therefore may we put our gold to work? My first investment was unfortunate, for I lost all. Its tale I will relate later. My first profitable investment was a loan I made to a man named Aggar, a shield maker. Once each year he bought large shipments of bronze brought from across the sea to use in his trade. Lacking sufficient capital to pay the merchants, he would borrow from those who had extra coins. He was an honorable man. His borrowing he would repay, together with a liberal rental, as he sold his shields.

"Each time I loaned to him I loaned back also the rental [interest] he had paid to me. Therefore not only did my capital increase, but its earnings likewise increased. Most gratifying was it to have these sums return to my wallet.

"I tell you, my students, a man's wealth is not in the coins he carries in his wallet; it is the income he builds, the golden stream that continually flows into his wallet and keeps it always bulging. That is what every man desires. That is what you, each one of you desires; an income that continues to come whether you work or travel.

"Great income I have acquired. So great that I am called a very rich man. My loans to Aggar were my first training in profitable investment. Gaining wisdom from this experience, I extended my loans and investments as my capital increased. From a few sources at first, from many sources later, flowed into my wallet a golden stream of wealth available for such wise uses as I should decide.

"Gold increases rapidly when making reasonable earnings as you will see from the following story:

"A farmer, when his first son was born, took ten pieces of silver to a money lender and asked him to keep it on rental [earning interest] for his son until he became twenty years of age. This the money lender did, and agreed the rental [interest] should be one-fourth of its value each four years. *The farmer asked,* because this sum he had set aside as belonging to his son, *that the rental [interest] be add to the principal.*

"When the boy had reached the age of twenty years, the farmer again went to the money lender to inquire about the silver. The money lender explained that *because this sum had been increased by compound interest, the original ten pieces of silver had now grown to thirty and one-half pieces.*

"The farmer was well pleased and because the son did not need the coins, he left them with the money lender. When the son became fifty years of age, the father meantime having passed to the other world, the money lender paid the son in settlement one hundred and sixty-seven pieces of silver. Thus in fifty years had the investment *multiplied itself at rental [interest] almost seventeen times.*

"This, then, is the **third cure** for a lean wallet: to put each coin to laboring that it may reproduce its kind even as the flocks of the field and help bring you income, a stream of wealth that shall flow constantly into your wallet."

Richest Ruminations

Gold in a wallet is gratifying to own and satisfies a miserly soul—but earns nothing. The gold you retain from your earnings is the start to building your fortune. How eager are you to learn how to make profitable investments?

What images come to your mind when you read the words, "...*wealth is not in the coins he carries in his wallet; it is the income he builds,* **the golden stream that continually flows into his wallet and keeps it always bulging.**"

Day 10

GUARD YOUR TREASURES

Misfortune loves a shining mark. Gold in a man's wallet must be guarded with firmness, else it be lost. Thus it is wise that we must first secure small amounts and learn to protect them before we're entrusted with larger." So spoke Arkad upon the fourth day to his class.

"Every owner of gold is tempted by opportunities whereby it would seem that he could make large sums by its investment in most plausible projects. Often friends and relatives are eagerly entering such investment and urge him to follow.

"*The first sound principle of investment is security for the principal.* Is it wise to be intrigued by larger earnings when your principal may be lost? I say not. The penalty of risk is probable loss. *Study carefully, before parting with your treasure,* each assurance that it may be safely reclaimed. Be not misled by your own romantic desires to make wealth rapidly.

"Before you loan it to anyone assure the person's ability to repay and his reputation for doing so, that you may not unwittingly be making him a present of thy hard-earned treasure. *"Before thou entrust it as an investment in any field acquaint thyself with the dangers which may beset it.*

"My own first investment was a tragedy to me at the time. The guarded savings of a year I did entrust to a brick maker, named Azmur, who was traveling over the far seas and agreed to buy for me the rare jewels of the Phoenicians. These we would sell upon his return and divide the profits. The Phoenicians were scoundrels and sold him bits of glass. My treasure was lost. Today, my training would show to me at once the folly of entrusting a brick maker to buy jewels.

"Therefore, do I advise thee from the wisdom of my experiences: be not too confident of your own wisdom in entrusting thy treasures to the possible pitfalls of investments. Better by far to consult the wisdom of those experienced in handling money for profit. Such advice is freely given for the asking and may readily possess a value equal in gold to the sum you considers investing. In truth, such is its actual value if it save thee from loss.

"This, then, is the **fourth cure** for a lean wallet, and of great importance to prevent your wallet from being emptied once it has become well filled. Guard thy treasure from loss by *investing only where thy principal is safe, where it may be reclaimed if desirable, and where thou will not fail to collect a fair rental.* Consult with wise men. *Secure the advice of those experienced in the profitable handling of finances.* Let their wisdom protect thy treasure from unsafe investments."

Richest Ruminations

Financial scammers are prevalent today. Have you been a victim? If yes, how could you have avoided the loss knowing now what you didn't know then?

If no, what measures will you take to keep from being tricked?

Money is governed today by the same laws which controlled it when prosperous people thronged the streets of Babylon, six thousand years ago.

Day 11

YOUR HOME, YOUR INVESTMENT

"If a man sets aside nine parts of his earnings upon which to live and enjoy life, and if any part of this nine parts he can turn into a profitable investment without detriment to his wellbeing, then so much faster will his treasures grow." So spake Arkad to his class at their fifth lesson.

"All too many of our men of Babylon raise their families in unseemly quarters. They pay to exacting landlords liberal rentals for rooms where their wives have not a spot to raise the blooms that gladden a woman's heart and their children have no place to play their games except in the unclean alleys.

"No man's family can fully enjoy life unless they have a plot of ground wherein children can play in the clean earth and where the wife may raise not only blossoms but good rich herbs to feed her family.

"To a man's heart it brings gladness to eat the figs from his own trees and the grapes of his own vines. To own his own domicile and to have it a place he is proud to care for, putteth confidence in his heart and greater effort behind all his endeavors. Therefore, do I recommend that every man own the roof that shelters him and his.

"Nor is it beyond the ability of any well intentioned man to own his home. Hath not our great king so widely extended the walls of Babylon that within them much land is now unused and may be purchased at sums most reasonable?

"Also I say to you, my students, that the money lenders gladly consider the desires of men who seek homes and land for their families. Readily may you borrow to pay the brick maker and the builder for such commendable purposes, if you can show a reasonable portion of the necessary sum that you provide for the purpose.

"Then when the house be built, you can pay the money lender with the same regularity as you paid the landlord. Because each payment will reduce thy indebtedness to the money lender, a few years will satisfy his loan.

"Then will your heart be glad because you wilt own in thy own right a valuable property and your only cost will be the king's taxes.

"Also wilt thy good wife go more often to the river to wash thy robes, that each time returning she may bring a goatskin of water to pour upon the growing things.

"Thus come many blessings to the man who owns his own house. And greatly will it reduce his cost of living, making available more of his earnings for pleasures and the gratification of his desires.

"This, then, is the **fifth cure** for a lean wallet: *Own your own home*"

Richest Ruminations

In addition to what Arkad told his class, list other advantages you see of owning your own home.

List the drawbacks of owning a home, and how you can overcome those obstacles.

Make your treasure work for you.

Day 12

FUTURE INCOME

The life of every man proceeds from his childhood to his old age. This is the path of life and no man may deviate from it. Therefore I say that it behooves a man to make preparation for a suitable income in the days to come, when he is no longer young, and to make preparations for his family should he be no longer with them to comfort and support them. This lesson shall instruct you in providing a full wallet when time has made you less able to learn." So Arkad addressed his class upon the sixth day.

"The man who, because of his understanding of the laws of wealth, acquires a growing surplus, should give thought to those future days. He should plan certain investments or provision that may endure safely for many years, yet will be available when the time arrives which he has so wisely anticipated.

"There are diverse ways by which a man may provide with safety for his future. He may provide a hiding place and there bury a secret treasure. Yet, no matter with what skill it be hidden, it may nevertheless become the loot of thieves. For this reason I do not recommend this plan.

"A man may *buy houses or lands* for this purpose. If wisely chosen as to their usefulness and value in the future, *they are permanent in their value and their earnings or their sale* will provide well for his purpose.

"A man may *loan a small sum to the money lender [bank, credit union, etc.] and increase it at regular periods.* The rental [interest] which the money lender adds to this will largely add to its increase. I know a sandal maker, named Ansan, who explained to me not long ago that each week for eight years he had deposited with his money lender two pieces of silver. The money lender had recently given him an accounting over which he greatly rejoiced. The total of his small deposits with their rental at the customary rate of one-fourth their value for each four years, had now become one thousand and forty pieces of silver.

"I did gladly encourage him further by demonstrating to him with my knowledge of the numbers that in twelve years more, if he would keep his regular deposits of but two pieces of silver each week, the money lender would then owe him four thousand pieces of silver, a worthy competence for the rest of his life.

"Surely, when such a small payment made with regularity produces such profitable results, no one can afford not to insure a treasure for his old age and the protection of his family, no matter how prosperous his business and his investments may be.

"I recommend to all men, that they, by wise and well thought out methods, do provide against a lean wallet in their mature years. For a lean wallet to a man no longer able to earn or to a family without its head is a sore tragedy.

"This, then, is the **sixth cure** for a lean wallet: Provide in advance for the needs of thy growing age and the protection of your family."

Richest Ruminations

Have you planned for your spouse and children's financial future if you pass sooner than expected? What steps will you take to secure a financially sound plan to provide for your family?

Do you see the importance of having a life insurance policy or of setting up a trust fund—or at the least having a Last Will and Testament set in place legally to ensure your wishes are known?

Counsel with the wise.

Day 13

EARN MORE

This day do I speak to thee, my students, of one of the most vital remedies for a lean wallet.

Yet, I will talk not of gold but of yourselves, of the men beneath the robes of many colors who do sit before me. I will talk to you of those things within the minds and lives of men which do work for or against their success." So did Arkad address his class upon the seventh day.

"Not long ago came to me a young man seeking to borrow. When I questioned him the cause of his necessity, he complained that his earnings were insufficient to pay his expenses. Thereupon I explained to him, this being the case, he was a poor customer for the money lender, as he possessed no surplus earning capacity to repay the loan.

"What you need, young man," I told him, "is to earn more coins. What do you do to increase your capacity to earn?"

"'All that I can do,' he replied. 'Six times within two moons have I approached my master to request my pay be increased, but without success. No man can go oftener than that.'

"We may smile at his simplicity, yet he did possess one of the vital requirements to increase his earnings. Within him was a strong desire to earn more, a proper and commendable desire.

"Preceding accomplishment must be desire. Your desires must be strong and definite. General desires are but weak longings. For a man to wish to be rich is of little purpose. For a man to desire five pieces of gold is a tangible desire which he can press to fulfillment. After he has backed his desire for five pieces of gold with strength of purpose to secure it, next he can find similar ways to obtain ten pieces and then twenty pieces and later a thousand pieces and, behold, he has become wealthy. In learning to secure his one definite small desire, he has trained himself to secure a larger one. This is the process by which wealth is accumulated: first in small sums, then in larger ones as a man learns and becomes more capable.

"*Desires must be simple and definite.* They defeat their own purpose should they be too many, too confusing, or beyond a man's training to accomplish." As a man perfects himself in his calling even so does his ability to earn increase.

"In those days when I was a humble scribe carving upon the clay for a few coppers each day, I observed that other workers did more than I and were paid more. Therefore, I determined that I would be exceeded by none. Nor did it take long for me to discover the reason for their greater success. More interest in my work, more concentration upon my task, more persistence in my effort, and, behold, few men could carve more tablets in a day than I. With reasonable promptness my increased skill was rewarded, nor was it necessary for me to go six times to my master to request recognition.

"The more of wisdom we know, the more we may earn. The man who seeks to learn more of his craft shall be richly rewarded. If he is an artisan, he may seek to learn the methods and the tools of those most skillful in the same line. If he labors at the law or at healing, he may consult and exchange knowledge with others of his calling. If he be a merchant, he may continually seek better goods that can be purchased at lower prices.

"Always do the affairs of man change and improve because keen-minded men seek greater skill that they may better serve those upon whose patronage they depend. Therefore, I urge all men to be in the front rank of progress and not to stand still, lest they be left behind.

"Many things come to make a man's life rich with gainful experiences. Such things as the following, a man must do if he respect himself:

"He must *pay his debts* with all the promptness within his power, not purchasing that for which he is unable to pay.

"He must *take care of his family* that they may think and speak well of him.

"He must *make a will of record* in case he passes unexpectedly so proper and honorable division of his property be accomplished.

"He must *have compassion* upon those who are injured and smitten by misfortune and aid them within reasonable limits. He must *do deeds of thoughtfulness* to those dear to him.

"Thus the **seventh and last remedy** for a lean wallet is to cultivate thy own powers, to study and become wiser, to become more skillful, to so act as to respect thyself. Thereby shalt thou acquire confidence in yourself to achieve your carefully considered desires.

"These then are the seven cures for a lean wallet, which, out of the experience of a long and successful life, I do urge for all men who desire wealth. There is more gold in Babylon, my students, than you dream of. There is abundance for all.

"Go forth and practice these truths that you may prosper and grow wealthy, as is your right. Go forth and teach these truths that every honorable subject of his majesty may also share liberally in the ample wealth of our beloved city."

Richest Ruminations

Have you determined to take more interest in your work, concentrate on your task, be more persistent in your effort—knowing that your increased skill will be rewarded?

Are you determined to earn more based on your desire to improve your skills and gain wisdom in your field of endeavor?

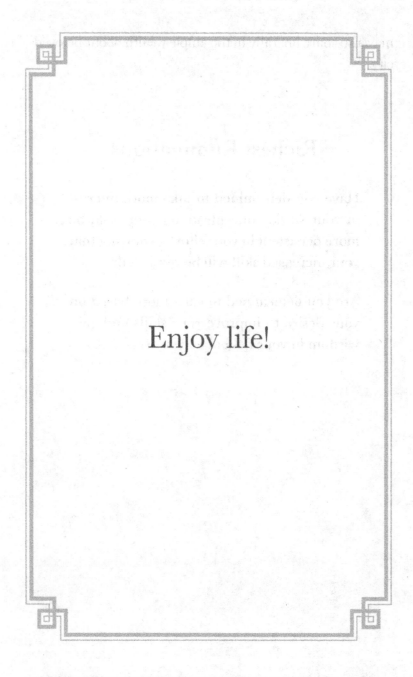

Enjoy life!

Day 14

GOOD BLESSINGS OR GOOD LUCK

If a man be lucky, there is no foretelling the possible extent of his good fortune. Pitch him into the Euphrates and like as not he will swim out with a pearl in his hand.

—Babylonian Proverb

Among the many who frequented the Temple of Learning, was a wise rich man named Arkad, called the richest man in Babylon. He had his own special hall where almost any evening a large group of men, some old, some very young, but mostly middle-aged, gathered to discuss and argue interesting subjects. Suppose we listen in to see whether they knew how to attract good luck.

The sun had just set like a great red ball of fire shining through the haze of desert dust when Arkad strolled to his accustomed platform. Already full four score men were awaiting his arrival, reclining on their small rugs spread upon the floor. More were still arriving.

"What shall we discuss this night?" Arkad inquired.

After a brief hesitation, a tall cloth weaver addressed him, arising as was the custom. "I have a subject I would like to hear discussed yet hesitate to offer lest it seem ridiculous to you, Arkad, and my good friends here."

Upon being urged to offer it, both by Arkad and by calls from the others, he continued: "This day I have been lucky, for I have found a wallet in which there are pieces of gold. To continue to be lucky is my great desire. Feeling that all men share with me this desire, I do suggest we debate how to attract good luck that we may discover ways it can be enticed to one."

"A most interesting subject has been offered," Arkad commented, "one most worthy of our discussion. To some men, good luck bespeaks but a chance happening that, like an accident, may befall one without purpose or reason. Others do believe that the instigator of all good fortune is a goddess."

Arkad continued, "To start our discussion, let us first hear from those among us who have enjoyed experiences similar to that of the cloth weaver in finding or receiving, without effort upon their part, valuable treasures or jewels."

There was a pause in which all looked about expecting someone to reply but no one did.

"What, no one?" Arkad said, "then rare indeed must be this kind of good luck. Who now will offer a suggestion as to where we shall continue our search?"

"That I will do," spoke a well-robed young man, arising. "When a man speaks of luck, is it not natural that his thoughts turn to the gaining tables? Is it not there we find many men courting the favour of the goddess in hope she will bless them with rich winnings?"

As he resumed his seat a voice called, "Do not stop! Continue the story! Tell us, did you find favor at the gaming tables? Did she turn the cubes with red side up so you filled your wallet at the dealer's expense or did she permit the blue sides to come up so the dealer raked in thy hard earned pieces of silver?"

The young man joined the good-natured laughter, then replied, "I am not averse to admitting she seemed not to know I was even there. But how about the rest of you? Have you found the goddess waiting about such places to roll the cubes, in your favor? We are eager to hear as well as to learn."

"A wise start," broke in Arkad. "We meet here to consider all sides of each question. To ignore the gaming table would be to overlook an instinct common to most men, the love of taking a chance with a small amount of silver in the hope of winning much gold."

Richest Ruminations

Do you depend on luck to bring you good fortune? Would you define good luck as a chance happening that, like an accident, may befall one without purpose or reason? Is there a difference between a "blessing from God" and "good luck from a goddess"?

Do you agree with the statement Arkad made that gambling is "an instinct common to most men, the love of taking a chance with a small amount of silver in the hope of winning much gold."

Day 15

CHANCES OF PROFIT

That reminds me of the races yesterday," called out another listener. "If the goddess frequents the gaming tables, certainly she does not overlook the races where the gilded chariots and the foaming horses offer far more excitement. Tell us honestly, Arkad, did she whisper to you to place your bet upon those grey horses from Nineveh yesterday? I was standing just behind you and could scarce believe my ears when I heard you place your bet upon the greys. You know as well as any of us that no team in all Assyria can beat our beloved bays in a fair race."

Arkad smiled indulgently at the banter. "What reason have we to feel a goddess would take that much interest in any man's bet upon a horse race? In tilling the soil, in honest trading, in all of man's occupations, there is opportunity to make a profit upon his efforts and his transactions.

"Perhaps not all the time will he be rewarded because sometimes his judgment may be faulty and other times the winds and the weather may defeat his efforts. Yet, if he persists, he may usually expect to realize his profit. This is so because the chances of profit are always in his favor.

"But, when a man plays the games, the situation is reversed for *the chances of profit are always against him* and always in favor of the game keeper. The game is so arranged that it will always favor the keeper. It is his business to plan to make a liberal profit for himself from the coins bet by the players. Few players realize how certain are the game keeper's profits and how uncertain are their own chances to win.

"Yet some men do win large sums at times," volunteered one of the listeners.

"Quite so, they do," Arkad continued. "Realizing this, the question comes to me whether money secured in such ways brings permanent value to those who are thus lucky. Among my acquaintances are many of the successful men of Babylon, yet among them *I am unable to name a single one who started his success from such a source as gambling.*

"You who are gathered here tonight know many more of our substantial citizens. To me it would be of much interest to learn how many of our successful citizens can credit the gaming tables with their start to success. Suppose each of you tell of those you know. What say you?"

After a prolonged silence, a wag ventured, "How about if the inquiry included the game keepers? If you think of no one else, surely they are the winners of the profit," Arkad responded.

"If not one of you can think of anyone else, then how about yourselves? Are there any consistent winners within us who hesitate to advise such a source for their incomes?"

His challenge was answered by a series of groans from the rear taken up and spread amid much laughter.

"It would seem we are not seeking good luck in such places as the goddess frequents," he continued. "Therefore let us explore other fields. We have not found it in picking up lost wallets.

Neither have we found it haunting the gaming tables. As to the races, I must confess to have lost far more coins there than I have ever won.

"Now, suppose we consider our trades and businesses. Is it not natural if we conclude a profitable transaction to consider it *not good luck but a just reward for our efforts?*"

Thereupon an elderly merchant arose, smoothing his genteel white robe.

"With thy permission, most honorable Arkad and my friends, I offer a suggestion. If, as you have said, we take credit to our own industry and ability for our business success, why not consider the successes we almost enjoyed but which escaped us, happenings which would have been most profitable. They would have been rare examples of good luck if they had actually happened. Because they were not brought to fulfillment we cannot consider them as our just rewards. Surely many men here have such experiences to relate."

Richest Ruminations

How many people do you know who are wealthy and have maintained their wealth actually started their success from such a source as gambling?

Would you rather take credit for your own ability and success than to give credit to the rare, if any, examples of good luck?

Day 16

LOSS AND LATER REGRET

"Here is a wise approach," Arkad approved. "Who among you have had good luck within your grasp only to see it escape?"

Many hands were raised, among them that of the merchant. Arkad motioned to him to speak. "As you suggested this approach, we should like to hear first from you."

"I will gladly relate a tale," he resumed, "that illustrates how closely unto a man opportunity may approach and how blindly he may permit it to escape, much to his loss and later regret.

"Many years ago, when I was a young man, just married and well-started to earning, my father came one day and urged most strongly that I enter into an investment. The son of one of his good friends had taken notice of a barren tract of land not far beyond the outer walls of our city. It lay high above the canal where no water could reach it.

"The son of my father's friend devised a plan to purchase this land, build three large water wheels that could be operated by oxen and thereby raise the life-giving waters to the fertile soil. This accomplished, he planned to divide into small tracts and sell to the residents of the city for herb patches.

"The son of my father's friend did not possess sufficient gold to complete such an undertaking. Like myself, he was a young man earning a fair sum. His father, like mine, was a man of large family and small means. He, therefore, decided to interest a group of men to enter the enterprise with him. The group was to comprise twelve, each of whom must be a money earner and agree to pay one-tenth of his earnings into the enterprise until the land was made ready for sale. All would then share justly in the profits in proportion to their investment."

"'You, my son,' bespoke my father unto me, 'are now in young manhood. It is my deep desire that you begin the building of a valuable estate for me that you may become respected among men. I desire to see you profit from a knowledge of the thoughtless mistakes of thy father.'

"This do I most ardently desire, my father," I replied.

"'Then, this do I advise. Do what I should have done at thy age. From thy earnings keep out one-tenth to put into favorable investments. *With this one-tenth of thy earnings* and what it will also earn, thou canst, before thou are my age, accumulate for yourself a valuable estate.'

"Thy words are words of wisdom, my father. Greatly do I desire riches. Yet there are many uses to which my earnings are called. Therefore, do I hesitate to do as you advise. I am young. There is plenty of time."

"So I thought at thy age, yet behold, many years have passed and I have not yet made the beginning.'

"We live in a different age, my father. I shall avoid thy mistakes."

'Opportunity stands before thee, my son. It is offering a chance that may lead to wealth. I beg of you, do not delay. Go tomorrow to the son of my friend and bargain with him to pay ten percent of thy earnings into this investment. Go promptly. *Opportunity waits for no man. Today it is here; soon it is gone. Therefore, delay not!*'

"In spite of the advice of my father, I did hesitate. There were beautiful new robes just brought by the tradesmen from the East, robes of such richness and beauty my good wife and I felt we must each possess one. Should I agree to pay one-tenth of my earnings into the enterprise, we must deprive ourselves of these and other pleasures we dearly desired. *I delayed making a decision until it was too late, much to my subsequent regret. The enterprise proved to be more profitable than anyone had prophesied.*

This is my tale, showing how I did permit good luck to escape."

"In this tale we see how fortune come to those who accept opportunity," commented a swarthy man of the desert. "To the building of an estate there must always be the beginning. That start may be a few pieces of gold or silver which a man diverts from his earnings to his first investment. I, myself, am the owner of many herds. The start of my herds I did begin when I was a mere boy and did purchase with one piece of silver a young calf. This, being the beginning of my wealth, was of great importance to me.

"To take his first start to building an estate is as good as can come to any man. With all men, that first step, which changes them from men who *earn from their own labor to men who draw dividends from the earnings of their gold, is important.* Some, fortunately, take it when young and thereby outstrip in financial success those who do take it later or those unfortunate men, like the father of this merchant, who never take it.

"Had our friend, the merchant, taken this step in his early manhood when this opportunity came to him, this day he would be blessed with much more of this world's goods. Should this story of our friend, the cloth weaver, cause him to take such a step at this time, it will indeed be the beginning of much greater good fortune."

Richest Ruminations

What opportunities did you allow to slip by because you weren't prepared? Afraid? Not willing to take the risk? Other reasons:

Do you actively look for opportunities to advance your financial status? Your career? Your relationships?

The best thing anyone can do is take that first step toward building wealth.

Day 17

THE POOR PROCRASTINATOR

"Thank you! I like to speak, also." A stranger from Syria arose. "I wish to call this friend, the merchant, a name. Maybe you think it not polite, yet I wish to call him a procrastinator. He accepts not opportunity when it comes. He waits. He says he has too much business right now, so bye and bye I talk to you later. Opportunity will not wait for such a slow fellow. If a man desires to be successful, he will step quickly. Any man who does not step quickly when opportunity comes, he is a procrastinator like our friend, this merchant."

The merchant arose and bowed good naturedly in response to the laughter.

"And now let us hear another tale of opportunity. Who has for us another experience?" demanded Arkad.

"I have," responded a red-robed man of middle age. "I am a buyer of animals, mostly camels and horses. Sometimes I also buy sheep and goats. The tale I am about to relate will tell truthfully how opportunity came one night when I least expected it. Perhaps for this reason I let it escape. Of this you shall be the judge.

"Returning to the city one evening after a disheartening ten-day journey in search of camels, I was much angered to find the gates of the city closed and locked. While my slaves spread our tent for the night, which we looked to spend with little food and no water, I was approached by an elderly farmer who, like ourselves, found himself locked outside.

"'Honored sir,' he addressed me, 'from thy appearance, I do judge you to be a buyer. If this be so, I would like to sell to you the most excellent flock of sheep just driven up. Alas, my good wife lies very sick with the fever. I must return with all haste. Buy my sheep so that I and my slaves may mount our camels and travel back home without delay.'

"So dark it was that I could not see his flock, but from the bleating I knew it must be large. Having wasted ten days searching for camels I could not find, I was glad to bargain with him. In his anxiety, he set a most reasonable price. I accepted, well knowing my slaves could drive the flock through the city gates in the morning and sell at a substantial profit.

"The bargain concluded, I called my slaves to bring torches that we might count the flock which the farmer declared to contain nine hundred. I shall not burden you, my friends, with a description of our difficulty in attempting to count so many thirsty, restless, milling sheep. It proved to be an impossible task. Therefore, I bluntly informed the farmer I would count them at daylight and pay him then.

"'Please, most honorable sir,' he pleaded, 'pay me but two-thirds of the price tonight that I may be on my way. I will leave my most intelligent and educated slave to assist to make the count in the morning. He is trustworthy and to him thou canst pay the balance.'

"But I was stubborn and refused to make payment that night. Next morning, before I awoke, the city gates opened and four buyers rushed out in search of flocks. They were most eager and willing to pay high prices because the city was threatened with siege, and food was not plentiful. Nearly three times the price at which he had offered the flock to me did the old farmer receive for it. Thus was the opportunity allowed to escape."

"Here is a tale most unusual," commented Arkad. "What wisdom does it suggest?"

"The wisdom of making a payment immediately when we are convinced our bargain is wise," suggested a venerable saddle maker. "If the bargain be good, then we need protection against our own weaknesses as much as against any other man. *We mortals are changeable. Alas, I must say more apt to change our minds when right than wrong. Wrong, we are stubborn indeed. Right, we are prone to vacillate and let opportunity escape.*

"My first judgment is my best. Yet always have I found it difficult to compel myself to proceed with a good bargain when made. Therefore, as a protection against my own weaknesses, I make a prompt deposit thereon. This saves me from later regrets for the good opportunity that should have been mine."

"Thank you! Again I like to speak," said the Syrian. "These tales are much alike. Each time opportunity flies away for same reason. Each time it comes to the procrastinator, bringing a good plan. But each time they hesitate, saying right now is not the best time. How can men succeed that way?"

"Wise are thy words, my friend," responded the buyer.

Richest Ruminations

Taking advantage of opportunities requires a wise and reasonably swift response. Waiting to make a decision likely results in a loss. How many good deals have you missed because you waited too long to respond?

Do you consider yourself a procrastinator? If yes, why are you prone to put off making decisions? Why do you delay choosing to take action?

Success comes to those
who act quickly on
a good opportunity,
as hesitation often
lets it slip away.

Day 18

PROFIT ROBBER

Procrastination was the key in both tales told in the previous two chapters. Yet, this is not unusual. The spirit of procrastination is within us all. We desire riches; yet, how often when opportunity appears before us, *that spirit of procrastination from within urges various delays in our acceptance. In listening to it we do become our own worst enemies.*

Said the merchant, "In my younger days I did not know it by this long word our friend from Syria exclaimed. I thought at first it was my own poor judgment that caused me loss of many profitable trades. Later, I credited it to my stubborn disposition. At last, I recognized it for what it was—a habit of needless delaying where action was required, action prompt and decisive. How I hate it when its true character stood revealed. With the bitterness of a wild ass hitched to a chariot, I broke loose from this enemy to my success."

The Syrian was spoke to the merchant, "You wear fine robes, not like those of poor man. You speak like successful man. Tell us, do you listen now when procrastination whispers in your ear?"

"I had to recognize and conquer procrastination," responded the merchant. "To me, it proved to be an enemy, ever watching and waiting to thwart my accomplishments. The tale I did relate is but one of many similar instances I could tell to show how it drove away my opportunities. Tis not difficult to conquer, once understood. No man willingly permits the thief to rob his bins of grain. Nor does any man willingly permit an enemy to drive away his customers and rob him of his profits. When once I recognized that such acts as these my enemy was committing, with determination I conquered him. *So must every man master his own spirit of procrastination before he can expect to share in the rich treasures* of Babylon.

"What sayest, Arkad? Because you are the richest man in Babylon, many proclaim thee to be the luckiest. Dost agree with me that no man can arrive at a full measure of success until he has completely crushed the spirit of procrastination within him?"

"It is even as you say," Arkad admitted. "During my long life I have watched generation following generation, marching forward along those avenues of trade, science, and learning that lead to success in life. Opportunities came to all these men. Some grasped theirs and moved steadily to the gratification of their deepest desires, but the majority hesitated, faltered and fell behind."

Arkad turned to the cloth weaver. "You suggested that we debate good luck. Let us hear what you now think upon the subject."

"I see good luck in a different light now. I had thought of it as something most desirable that might happen to a man without effort upon his part. Now, I realize such happenings are not the sort of thing one may attract to himself. From our discussion have I learned that it is necessary to take advantage of opportunities. Therefore, in the future, I shall endeavor to make the best of such opportunities as do come to me."

"Thou hast well grasped the truths brought forth in our discussion," Arkad replied. "Our merchant friend would have found great success had he accepted the opportunity. Our friend the buyer, likewise, would have enjoyed good fortune had he completed the purchase of the flock and sold at such a handsome profit.

"We pursued this discussion to find a means by which success could be enticed to us. I feel that we have found the way. Both the tales did illustrate how success follows opportunity. Herein lies a truth that many similar tales of won or lost could not change: Success can be enticed by accepting opportunity.

"Those eager to grasp opportunities for their betterment, attract success. Action will lead thee forward to the successes you desire."

Richest Ruminations

Would you agree that the spirit of procrastination from within urges hesitations and delays making critical decisions? And do you agree that by listening to that spirit we become our own worst enemies?

Success can be enticed by accepting opportunity. True?

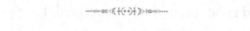

Day 19

FIVE LAWS OF GOLD

For the benefit of you who are seated here this night, I will read the wisdom of my father as engraved upon the clay tablet which he gave to me ten years ago:

The Five Laws of Gold

1. Gold cometh gladly and in increasing quantity to any man who will put by not less than one-tenth of his earnings to create an estate for his future and that of his family.
2. Gold laboreth diligently and contentedly for the wise owner who finds for it profitable employment, multiplying even as the flocks of the field.
3. Gold clingeth to the protection of the cautious owner who invests it under the advice of men wise in its handling.

4. Gold slippeth away from the man who invests it in businesses or purposes with which he is not familiar or which are not approved by those skilled in its keep.
5. Gold flees the man who would force it to impossible earnings or who followeth the alluring advice of tricksters and schemers or who trusts it to his own inexperience and romantic desires in investment.

"These are the five laws of gold as written by my father. I do proclaim them as of greater value than gold itself.

"Because I learned these five laws in my youth and abided by them, I have become a wealthy merchant. Not by some strange magic did I accumulate my wealth.

"Wealth that comes quickly goes the same way.

"Wealth that stays to give enjoyment and satisfaction to its owner comes gradually, because it is a child born of knowledge and persistent purpose.

"To earn wealth is but a slight burden upon the thoughtful person. Bearing the burden consistently from year to year accomplishes the final purpose.

"The five laws of gold offer to you a rich reward for their observance. Each of these five laws is rich with meaning. I know them each by heart because in my youth, I could see their value and would not be content until I knew them word for word."

Richest Ruminations

Which of the five laws will be the easiest to establish into your everyday lifestyle? The hardest?

Which of the five laws of gold do you deem the most important? The least important?

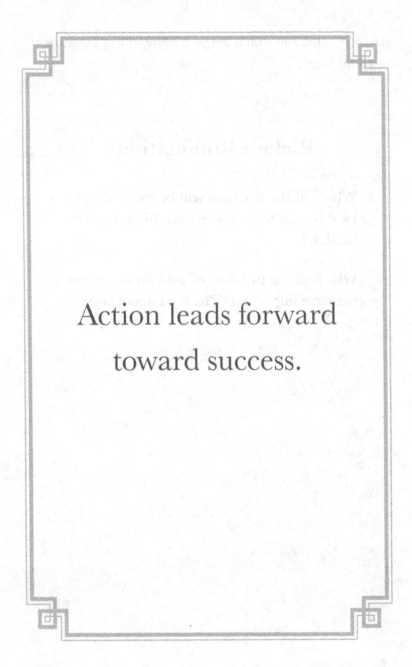

Action leads forward toward success.

Day 20

BEWARE

Know that:
"Gold flees the man who would force it to impossible earnings or who follows the alluring advice of tricksters and schemers or who trusts it to his own inexperience and romantic desires in investment.

"Fanciful propositions that thrill like adventure tales always come to the new owner of gold. These appear to endow his treasure with powers that enable it to make impossible earnings. Yet heed ye the wise men, for verily they know the risks that lurk behind every plan to make great wealth suddenly.

"Forget not the rich men of Nineveh who would take no chance of losing their principal or tying it up in unprofitable investments.

"In telling you the five laws of gold, I have told the secrets of my own success.

"Yet, they are not secrets but truths every man must first learn and then follow who wishes to step out of the multitude that, like wild dogs, must worry each day for food to eat."

Ten years from this night, what can you tell about this gold?

If there be men among you, who will use a portion of their gold to start for themselves an estate and be thenceforth wisely guided by the wisdom of Arkad, ten years from now, 'tis a safe wager, like the son of Arkad, they will be rich and respected among men.

Our wise acts accompany us through life to please us and to help us. Just as surely, our unwise acts follow us to plague and torment us. Alas, they cannot be forgotten. In the front rank of the torments that do follow us are the memories of the things we should have done, of the opportunities which came to us and we took not.

Rich are the treasures of Babylon, so rich no man can count their value in pieces of gold. Each year, they grow richer and more valuable. Like the treasures of every land, they are a reward, a rich reward awaiting those men of purpose who determine to secure their just share.

In the strength of thine own desires is a power. Guide this power with thy knowledge of the five laws of gold and you shall share the treasures of Babylon.

Richest Ruminations

Will you follow the five laws of gold starting today? Are you prepared to tackle the commitment it takes to move you toward your financial goals and claim them accomplished?

"Gold flees the man who would force it to impossible earnings or who follows the alluring advice of tricksters and schemers or who trusts it to his own inexperience and romantic desires in investment." What does this sentence mean to you? Write it in your own words:

Wealth escapes those who chase unrealistic profits, fall for scams, and rely on inexperience, but grows for those who wisely invest their money.

Day 21

THE GOLD LENDER

Fifty pieces of gold! Never before had Rodan, the spear maker of old Babylon, carried so much gold in his leather wallet. Happily down the king's highway from the palace of his most liberal majesty he strode. Cheerfully the gold clinked as the wallet at his belt swayed with each step—the sweetest music he had ever heard.

Fifty pieces of gold! All his! He could hardly realize his good fortune. What power in those clinking discs! They could purchase anything he wanted, a grand house, land, cattle, camels, horses, chariots, whatever he might desire.

What use should he make of it? This evening as he turned into a side street towards the home of his sister, he could think of nothing he would rather possess than those same glittering, heavy pieces of gold—his to keep.

It was upon an evening some days later that a perplexed Rodan entered the shop of Mathon, the lender of gold and dealer in jewels and rare fabrics. Glancing neither to the right nor the left at the colorful articles artfully displayed, he passed through to the living quarters at the rear. Here he found the genteel Mathon lounging upon a rug partaking of a meal.

"I would counsel with thee for I know not what to do." Rodan stood stolidly, feet apart, hairy chest exposed by the gaping front of his leather jacket. Mathon's narrow, sallow face smiled a friendly greeting. "What indiscretions hast thou done that thou shouldst seek the lender of gold? Hast been unlucky at the gaming table? Or hath some plump dame entangled thee? For many years have I known thee, yet never hast thou sought me to aid thee in thy troubles."

"No, no. Not such as that. I seek no gold. Instead I crave thy wise advice."

"Hear! Hear! What this man doth say. No one comes to the lender of gold for advice. My ears must play me false."

"They listen true."

"Can this be so? Rodan, the spear maker, displays more cunning than all the rest, for he comes to Mathon, not for gold, but for advice. Many men come to me for gold to pay for their follies, but as for advice, they want it not. Yet who is more able to advise than the lender of gold to whom many men come in trouble?

"Thou shalt eat with me, Rodan," he continued. Thou shalt be my guest for the evening. Andol," he commanded of the slave, "draw up a rag for my friend, Rodan, the spear maker, who comes for advice. He shall be my honored guest. Bring to him much food and get for him my largest cup. Choose well of the best wine that he may have satisfaction in the drinking. Now, tell me what troubles thee."

"It is the king's gift."

"The king's gift? The king gave you a gift and it gives you trouble? What manner of gift?"

"Because he was much pleased with the design I did submit to him for a new point on the spears of the royal guard, he presented me with fifty pieces of gold, and now I am much perplexed. I am asked each hour the sun travels across the sky by those who want to share it with me."

"That is natural. More men want gold than have it, and would wish one who comes by it easily to divide. But can you not say 'No?' Is thy will not as strong as thy fist?"

"To many I can say no, yet sometimes it would be easier to say yes. Can one refuse to share with one's sister to whom he is deeply devoted?"

"Surely, thy own sister would not wish to deprive you of enjoying your reward."

"But it is for the sake of Araman, her husband, whom she wishes to see as a rich merchant. She feels that he has never had a chance and she beseeches me to loan to him this gold that he may become a prosperous merchant and repay me from his profits."

"My friend," resumed Mathon, "tis a worthy subject you bring to discuss. Gold brings unto its possessor responsibility and a changed position with his fellow men. It brings fear lest he lose it or it be tricked away from him. It brings a feeling of power and ability to do good. Likewise, it brings opportunities whereby his very good intentions may bring him into difficulties."

Richest Ruminations

Have you been the recipient of a large financial gift and you weren't quite sure how to handle it? Did you seek advice from a spouse, friend, coworker, financial adviser?

If you did receive such a gift, were you happy with how you chose to handle the windfall? Looking back would you have made other decisions knowing what you know now?

Day 22

BORROWING AND LENDING

Mathon continued speaking to distressed Rodan, "Did you ever hear of the farmer of Nineveh who could understand the language of animals? I doubt you have, for 'tis not the kind of tale men like to tell over the bronze caster's forge. I will tell it to you for you should know that to borrowing and lending there is more than the passing of gold from the hands of one to the hands of another.

"This farmer, who could understand what the animals said to each other, did linger in the farm yard each evening just to listen to their words. One evening he heard the ox bemoaning to the ass the hardness of his lot: 'I labor pulling the plow from morning until night. No matter how hot the day, or how tired my legs, or how the bow chafes my neck, still must I work. But you are a creature of leisure. You are trapped with a colorful blanket and do nothing more than carry our master where he wishes to go. When he goes nowhere you rest and eat the green grass all the day.'

"Now the ass, in spite of his vicious heels, was a goodly fellow and sympathized with the ox. 'My good friend,' he replied, 'you do work very hard and I would help ease your lot. Therefore, will I tell you how you may have a day of rest. In the morning when the slave comes to fetch you to the plow, lie upon the ground and bellow much that he may say you are sick and cannot work.'

"So the ox took the advice of the ass and the next morning the slave returned to the farmer and told him the ox was sick and could not pull the plow.

"'Then,' said the farmer, 'hitch the ass to the plow for the plowing must go on.'

"All that day the ass, who had only intended to help his friend, found himself compelled to do the ox's task. When night came and he was released from the plow his heart was bitter and his legs were weary and his neck was sore where the bow had chafed it.

"The farmer lingered in the barnyard to listen.

"The ox began first. 'You are my good friend. Because of your wise advice I have enjoyed a day of rest.'

"'And I,' retorted the ass, 'am like many another simple-hearted one who starts to help a friend and ends up by doing his task for him. Hereafter you draw your own plow, for I did hear the master tell the slave to send for the butcher were you sick again. I wish he would, for you are a lazy fellow.' Thereafter they spoke to each other no more—this ended their friendship. Can you tell the moral to this tale, Rodan?"

"Tis a good tale," responded Rodan, "but I see not the moral."

"I thought you would not. But it is there and simple too. Just this: If you desire to help your friend, do so in a way that will not bring your friend's burdens upon yourself."

"I had not thought of that. It is a wise moral. I wish not to assume the burdens of my sister's husband. But tell me. You lend to many. Do not the borrowers repay?"

Mathon smiled the smile of one whose soul is rich with much experience.

"Could a loan be well made if the borrower cannot repay? Must not the lender be wise and judge carefully whether his gold can perform a useful purpose to the borrower and return to him once more; or whether it will be wasted by one unable to use it wisely and leave him without his treasure, and leave the borrower with a debt he cannot repay? I will show you tokens in my token chest and let them tell you some of their stories."

Into the room he brought a chest as long as his arm covered with red pigskin and ornamented with bronze designs. He placed it upon the floor and squatted before it, both hands upon the lid.

"From each person to whom I lend, I do exact a token for my token chest, to remain there until the loan is repaid. When they repay I give back, but if they never repay it will always remind me of one who was not faithful to my confidence.

"The safest loans, my token box tells me, are to those whose possessions are of more value than the one they desire. They own lands, or jewels, or camels, or other things which could be sold to repay the loan. Some of the tokens given to me are jewels of more value than the loan. Others are promises that if the loan be not repaid as agreed they will deliver to me certain property settlement. On loans like those I am assured that my gold will be returned with the rental thereon, for the loan is based on property."

Richest Ruminations

"If you desire to help your friend, do so in a way that will not bring your friend's burdens upon yourself." Did the moral to this story bring back memories of an unwise loan you made and later regretted?

Have you assumed the financial burden of someone close to you and later had regrets because you realized the loan will not be repaid? How can you avoid this situation in the future?

If you want to help
a friend financially,
do so in a way that
doesn't leave you
carrying their burden.

Day 23

HUMAN-EFFORT LOANS

Mathon continued, "In another class are those who have the capacity to earn. They are such as you, who labor or serve and are paid. They have income and if they are honest and suffer no misfortune, I know they also can repay the gold I loan them and the rental [interest] to which I am entitled. Such loans are based on human effort.

"Others are those who have neither property nor assured earning capacity. Life is hard and there will always be some who cannot adjust themselves to it. Alas for the loans I make them, even though they be no larger than a pence, my token box may censure me in the years to come unless they be guaranteed by good friends of the borrower who know him as honorable."

Mathon released the clasp and opened the lid. Rodan leaned forward eagerly.

At the top of the chest a bronze neck-piece lay upon a scarlet cloth. Mathon picked up the piece and patted it affectionately. "This shall always remain in my token chest because the owner has passed on. I treasure it, his token, and I treasure his memory; for he was my good friend. We traded together with much success until out of the east he brought a woman to wed, beautiful, but not like our women. A dazzling creature. He spent his gold lavishly to gratify her desires.

"He came to me in distress when his gold was gone. I counseled with him. I told him I would help him to once more master his own affairs. He swore that he would. But it was not to be. In a quarrel she thrust a knife into the heart he dared her to pierce."

"And she?" questioned Rodan.

"Yes, of course, this was hers." He picked up the scarlet cloth. "In bitter remorse she threw herself into the Euphrates. These two loans will never be repaid. The chest tells you, Rodan, that humans in the throes of great emotions are not safe risks for the gold lender.

"Here! Now this is different." He reached for a ring carved of ox bone. "This belongs to a farmer. I buy the rugs of his women. The locusts came and they had no food. I helped him and when the new crop came he repaid me. Later he came again and told of strange goats in a distant land as described by a traveler. They had long hair so fine and soft it would weave into rugs more beautiful than any ever seen in Babylon. He wanted a herd but he had no money. So I did lend him gold to make the journey and bring back goats. Now his herd is begun and next year I shall surprise the lords of Babylon with the most expensive rugs it has been their good fortune to buy. Soon I must return his ring. He insists on repaying promptly."

"Some borrowers do that?' queried Rodan.

"If they borrow for purposes that bring money back to them, I find it so. But if they borrow because of their indiscretions, I warn thee to be cautious if thou wouldst ever have thy gold back in hand again."

"Tell me about this," requested Rodan, picking up a heavy gold bracelet inset with jewels in rare designs.

"The women do appeal to my good friend," bantered Mathon.

"I am still much younger than you," retorted Rodan.

"I grant that, but this time you suspect romance where it is not. The owner of this is fat and wrinkled and talks so much and says so little she drives me mad. Once they had much money and were good customers, but ill times came upon them. She has a son of whom she would make a merchant. So she came to me and borrowed gold that he might become a partner of a caravan owner who travels with his camels bartering in one city what he buys in another.

"This man proved a rascal for he left the poor boy in a distant city without money and without friends, pulling out early while the youth slept. Perhaps when this youth has grown to manhood, he will repay; until then I get no rental for the loan—only much talk. But I do admit the jewels are worthy of the loan."

"Did this lady ask your advice as to the wisdom of the loan to her son?"

"Quite otherwise. She had pictured to herself this son of hers as a wealthy and powerful man of Babylon. To suggest the contrary was to infuriate her. A fair rebuke I had. I knew the risk for this inexperienced boy, but as she offered security I could not refuse her.

"This," continued Mathon, waving a bit of pack rope tied into a knot, "belongs to Nebatur, the camel trader. When he would buy a herd larger than his funds he brings to me this knot and I lend to him according to his needs. He is a wise trader. I have confidence in his good judgment and can lend to him freely. Many other merchants of Babylon have my confidence because of their honorable behavior. Their tokens come and go frequently in my token box. Good merchants are an asset to our city and it profits me to aid them to keep trade moving that Babylon makes prosperous."

Richest Ruminations

It was written that "humans in the throes of great emotions are not safe risks for the gold lender," do you know that to be true? Are you prone to make good or bad decisions when emotionally fraught?

To whom would you lend financial aid if asked?

Lend money wisely.

Day 24

HOPELESS DEBT

Mathon picked out a beetle carved in turquoise and tossed it contemptuously on the floor. "A bug from Egypt. The lad who owns this does not care whether I ever receive back my gold. When I reproach him he replies, 'How can I repay when ill fate pursues me? You have plenty more.' What can I do? The token is his father's—a worthy man of small means who did pledge his land and herd to back his son's enterprises. The youth found success at first and then was overzealous to gain great wealth. His knowledge was immature. His enterprises collapsed.

"Youth is ambitious. Youth take short cuts to wealth and the desirable things for which it stands. To secure wealth quickly youth often borrows unwisely. Youth, never having had experience, cannot realize that hopeless debt is like a deep pit into which one may descend quickly and where one may struggle vainly for many days. It is a pit of sorrow and regrets where the brightness of the sun is overcast and night is made unhappy by restless sleeping. Yet, I do not discourage borrowing gold. I encourage it. I recommend it if it be for a wise purpose. I myself made my first real success as a merchant with borrowed gold.

"Yet, what should the lender do in such a case? The youth is in despair and accomplishes nothing. He is discouraged. He makes no effort to repay. My heart turns against depriving the father of his land and cattle."

"You tell me much that I am interested to hear," ventured Rodan, "but, I hear no answer to my question. Should I lend my fifty pieces of gold to my sister's husband? They mean much to me."

"Your sister is a sterling woman whom I do much esteem. Should her husband come to me and ask to borrow fifty pieces of gold I should ask him for what purpose he would use it. If he answered that he desired to become a merchant like myself and deal in jewels and rich furnishings. I would say, 'What knowledge have you of the ways of trade? Do you know where you can buy at lowest cost? Do you know where you can sell at a fair price?" Could he say 'Yes' to these questions?"

"No, he could not," Rodan admitted. "He has helped me much in making spears and he has helped some in the shops."

"Then, would I say to him that his purpose was not wise. Merchants must learn their trade. His ambition, though worthy, is not practical and I would not lend him any gold.

"But, supposing he could say: 'Yes, I have helped merchants much. I know how to travel to Smyrna and to buy at low cost the rugs the housewives weave. I also know many of the rich people of Babylon to whom I can sell these at a large profit.' Then I would say: 'Your purpose is wise and your ambition honorable. I shall be glad to lend you the fifty pieces of gold if you can give me security that they will be returned.'"

"But would he say, 'I have no security other than that I am an honored man and will pay you well for the loan.' Then would I reply, 'I treasure much each piece of gold. Were the robbers to take it from you as you journeyed to Smyrna or take the rugs from you as you returned, then you would have no means of repaying me and my gold would be gone.'

"Gold, you see, Rodan, is the merchandise of the lender of money. It is easy to lend. If it is lent unwisely then it is difficult to get back. The wise lender wishes not the risk of the undertaking but the guarantee of safe repayment.

"'Tis well," he continued, "to assist those who are in trouble, tis well to help those upon whom fate has laid a heavy hand. Tis well to help those who are starting that they may progress and become valuable citizens. But help must be given wisely, lest, like the farmer's ass, in our desire to help we but take upon ourselves the burden that belongs to another."

Richest Ruminations

As a young person, were you ambitious, did you take shortcuts to get what you wanted, have you lost sleep because of your debts?

Are you as wise as Mathon regarding loaning money to people? Do you weigh the risks before making the decision?

Day 25

SECRETS OF THE TOKEN CHEST

Again I wandered from your question, Rodan, but hear my answer: Keep your fifty pieces of gold. What your labor earns for you and what is given to you for reward is your own and no man can put an obligation upon you to part with it unless it is your wish. If you lend it so that it may earn you more gold, then lend with caution and in many places. I like not idle gold, even less I like too much risk.

"How many years hast thou labored as a spear maker?"

"Fully three."

"How much besides the King's gift have you saved?"

"Three gold pieces."

"Each year that you labored you has denied yourself good things to save from your earnings one piece of gold?"

"Tis as you say."

"Then mightest save in fifty years of labor fifty pieces of gold by thy self-denial?"

"A lifetime of labor it would be."

"Think, would your sister wish to jeopardize the savings of fifty years of labor over the bronze melting pot that her husband might experiment on being a merchant?"

"Not if I spoke in your words."

"Then go to her and say: 'Three years I have labored each day except fast days, from morning until night, and I have denied myself many things that my heart craved. For each year of labor and self-denial I have to show one piece of gold. You are my favored sister and I wish that your husband may engage in business in which he will prosper greatly. If he will submit to me a plan that seems wise and possible to my friend, Mathon, then will I gladly lend to him my savings of an entire year that he may have an opportunity to prove that he can succeed.' Do that, I say, and if he has within him the soul to succeed he can prove it. If he fails he will not owe thee more than he can hope some day to repay.

"I am a gold lender because I own more gold than I can use in my own trade. I desire my surplus gold to labor for others and thereby earn more gold. I do not wish to take risk of losing my gold for I have labored much and denied myself much to secure it. Therefore, I will no longer lend any of it where I am not confident that it is safe and will be returned to me. Neither will I lend it where I am not convinced that its earnings will be promptly paid to me.

"I have told to thee, Rodan, a few of the secrets of my token chest. From them you may understand the weakness of men and their eagerness to borrow that which they have no certain means to repay. From this you can see how often their high hopes of the great earnings they could make, if they but had gold, are but false hopes they have not the ability or training to fulfill.

"You, Rodan, now have gold that you should put to earning more gold for yourself. You are about to become as I, a gold lender. If you safely preserve your treasure it will produce liberal earnings and be a rich source of pleasure and profit during all thy days. But if you let it escape, it will be a source of constant sorrow and regret as long as thy memory doth last.

"Therefore, be not swayed by the fantastic plans of impractical men who think they see ways to force thy gold to make earnings unusually large. Such plans are the creations of dreamers unskilled in the safe and dependable laws of trade. Be conservative in what thou expect it to earn that thou mayest keep and enjoy thy treasure. To hire it out with a promise of exorbitant returns is to invite loss.

"Associate with men and enterprises whose success is established that thy treasure may earn liberally under their skillful use and be guarded safely by their wisdom and experience.

When Rodan thanked Mathon for his wise advice he would not listen, saying, "The king's gift shall teach you much wisdom. If you keep your fifty pieces of gold you must be discreet indeed.

Many uses will tempt thee. Much advice will be spoken. Numerous opportunities to make large profits will be offered. The stories from my token box should warn you, before you let any piece of gold to leave your pouch, be sure you have a safe way to pull it back again. Should my further advice appeal to you, return again. It is gladly given.

"Before you go, read this which I have carved beneath the lid of my token box. It applies equally to the borrower and the lender: *Better a little caution than a great regret.*"

Richest Ruminations

"Your reward is your own. If you lend it so that it may earn you more gold, then lend with caution and in many places. I like not idle gold, even less I like too much risk." Is this advice you will take seriously?

How does your personality sync with this advice about lending finances, even to a family member?

Better a little caution than a great regret.

Day 26

BABYLON'S WALLS

Old Banzar, grim warrior of another day, stood guard at the passageway leading to the top of the ancient walls of Babylon. Up above, valiant defenders were battling to hold the walls from enemies. Upon them depended the future existence of this great city with its hundreds of thousands of citizens.

Over the walls came the roar of the attacking armies, the yelling of many men, the trampling of thousands of horses, the deafening boom of the battering rams pounding the bronzed gates.

In the street behind the gate lounged the spearmen, waiting to defend the entrance should the gates give way. They were but few for the task. The main armies of Babylon were with their king, far away in the east on the great expedition against the Elamites. No attack upon the city having been anticipated during their absence, the defending forces were small.

Unexpectedly, from the north, bore down the mighty armies of the Assyrians. And now the walls must hold or Babylon was doomed.

Around Banzar were great crowds of citizens, white-faced and terrified, eagerly seeking news of the battle. With hushed awe they viewed the stream of wounded and dead being carried or led out of the passageway. Here was the crucial point of attack. After three days of circling around the city, the enemy had suddenly thrown his great strength against this section and this gate.

The defenders from the top of the wall fought off the climbing platforms and the scaling ladders of the attackers with arrows, burning oil and, if any reached the top, spears. Against the defenders, thousands of the enemy's archers poured a deadly barrage of arrows.

Old Banzar had the vantage point for news. He was closest to the conflict and first to hear of each fresh repulse of the frenzied attackers.

An elderly merchant crowded close to him, his palsied hands quivering. "Tell me! Tell me!" he pleaded. "They cannot get in. My sons are with the good king. There is no one to protect my old wife. My goods, they will steal all. My food, they will leave nothing. We are old, too old to defend ourselves—too old for slaves. We shall starve. We shall die. Tell me they cannot get in."

"Calm thyself, good merchant," the guard responded. "The walls of Babylon are strong. Go back to the bazaar and tell your wife that the walls will protect you and all of your possessions as safely as they protect the rich treasures of the king. Keep close to the walls, lest the arrows flying over strike you!"

A woman with a babe in arms took the old man's place as he withdrew.

"Sergeant, what news from the top? Tell me truly that I may reassure my poor husband. He lies with fever from his terrible wounds, yet insists upon his armor and his spear to protect me, who am with child. Terrible he says will be the vengeful lust of our enemies should they break in."

"Be thou of good heart, thou mother who is, and is again to be, the walls of Babylon will protect you and your babes. They are high and strong. Hear ye not the yells of our valiant defenders as they empty the caldrons of burning oil upon the ladder scalers?"

"Yes, that do I hear and also the roar of the battering rams that do hammer at our gates."

"Back to thy husband. Tell him the gates are strong and withstand the rams. Also that the scalers climb the walls but to receive the waiting spear thrust. Watch your way and hasten to go behind the buildings."

Banzar stepped aside to clear the passage for heavily armed reinforcements. As with clanking bronze shields and heavy tread they tramped by, a small girl plucked at his cloak. "Tell me please, soldier, are we safe?" she pleaded. I hear the awful noises. I see the men all bleeding. I am so frightened. What will become of our family, of my mother, little brother, and the baby?"

The grim old campaigner blinked his eyes and thrust forward his chin as he beheld the child.

"Be not afraid, little one," he reassured her. "The walls of Babylon will protect you and mother and little brother and the baby. It was for the safety of such as you that the good Queen Semiramis built them over a hundred years ago. Never have they been broken through. Go back and tell your mother and little brother and the baby that the walls of Babylon will protect them and they need have no fear."

Richest Ruminations

Do you have walls of protection around you, your family, your finances, your job, your home? How reassuring are you when danger approaches?

How strong are your gates and do those in your circle feel safe and secure knowing you are at the helm? That you will do everything possible to bring peace and stability?

Stay calm and trust in the strength of our defenses, as they will keep you and your loved ones safe from harm.

Day 27

FULLY PROTECTED

Day after day old Banzar stood at his post and watched the reinforcements file up the passageway, there to stay and fight until wounded or dead they came down once more. Around him, unceasingly crowded the throngs of frightened citizens eagerly seeking to learn if the walls would hold. To all he gave his answer with the fine dignity of an old soldier, "The walls of Babylon will protect you."

For three weeks and five days the attack waged with scarcely ceasing violence. Harder and grimmer set the jaw of Banzar as the passage behind, wet with the blood of the many wounded, was churned into mud by the never ceasing streams of men passing up and staggering down.

Each day the slaughtered attackers piled up in heaps before the wall. Each night they were carried back and buried by their comrades. Upon the fifth night of the fourth week the clamor diminished. The first streaks of daylight, illuminating the plains, disclosed great clouds of dust raised by the retreating armies.

A mighty shout went up from the defenders. There was no mistaking its meaning. It was repeated by the waiting troops behind the walls. It was echoed by the citizens upon the streets. It swept over the city with the violence of a storm.

People rushed from the houses. The streets were jammed with a throbbing mob. The pent-up fear of weeks found an outlet in the wild chorus of joy. From the top of the high tower of the Temple of Bel burst forth the flames of victory. Skyward floated the column of blue smoke to carry the message far and wide.

The walls of Babylon had once again repulsed a mighty and viscous foe determined to loot her rich treasures and to ravish and enslave her citizens. Babylon endured century after century because it was fully protected. It could not afford to be otherwise.

The walls of Babylon were an outstanding example of man's need and desire for protection.

This desire is inherent in the human race. It is just as strong today as it ever was, but we have developed broader and better plans to accomplish the same purpose.

In this day, behind the impregnable walls of insurance, savings accounts and dependable investments, we can guard ourselves against the unexpected tragedies that may enter any door and seat themselves before any fireside.

Richest Ruminations

Hope is what Banzar gave the people who were frenzied with fear. Are you so sure of your stance that you can give hope to those in need? Who are searching for a victory?

Today, we can live fully protected behind walls of insurance, savings accounts, and dependable investments. Have you provided safeguards against unexpected circumstances that may arrive?

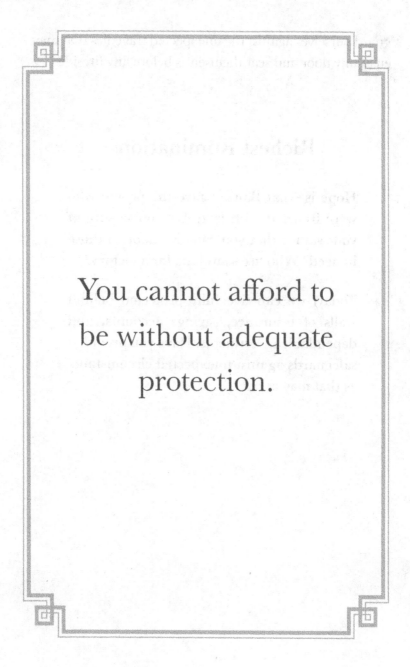

You cannot afford to be without adequate protection.

Day 28

A DIFFERENT COLOR OF LIFE

For two whole days Azure had tasted no food except two small figs purloined from over the wall of a garden. Not another could he grab before the angry woman rushed forth and chased him down the street. Her shrill cries were still ringing in his ears as he walked through the market place. They helped him to retrain his restless fingers from snatching the tempting fruits from the baskets of the market women.

Never before had he realized how much food was brought to the markets of Babylon and how good it smelled. Leaving the market, he walked across to the inn and paced back and forth in front of the eating house. Perhaps here he might meet someone he knew; someone from whom he could borrow a copper that would gain him a smile from the unfriendly keeper of the inn and, with it, a liberal helping. Without the copper he knew all too well how unwelcome he would be.

In his abstraction he unexpectedly found himself face to face with the one man he wished most to avoid, the tall bony figure of Dabasir, the camel trader. Of all the friends and others from whom he had borrowed small sums, Dabasir made him feel the most uncomfortable because of his failure to keep his promises to repay promptly.

Dabasir's face lit up at the sight of him. "Ha! Tis Tarkad, just the one I have been seeking that he might repay the two pieces of copper I lent him a moon ago; also the piece of silver I lent to him before that. We are well met. I can make good use of the coins this very day. What say, boy? What say?"

Tarkad stuttered and his face flushed. He had nothing in his empty stomach to nerve him to argue with the outspoken Dabasir. "I am sorry, very sorry," he mumbled weakly, "but this day I have neither the copper nor the silver with which I could repay."

"Then get it," Dabasir insisted. "Surely thou can get hold of a few coppers and a piece of silver to repay the generosity of an old friend of thy father who aided you when you were in need?"

"Tis because ill fortune does pursue me that I cannot pay."

"Ill fortune! Wouldst blame the gods for thine own weakness. Ill fortune pursues every man who thinks more of borrowing than of repaying. Come with me, boy, while I eat. I am hungry and I'll tell you a tale."

Tarkad flinched from the brutal frankness of Dabasir, but here at least was an invitation to enter the coveted doorway of the eating house.

Dabasir pushed him to a far corner of the room where they seated themselves upon small rugs.

When Kauskor, the proprietor, appeared smiling, Dabasir addressed him with his usual freedom, "Fat lizard of the desert, bring to me a leg of the goat, brown with much juice, and bread and all of the vegetables for I am hungry and want much food. Do not forget my friend here. Bring to him a jug of water. Have it cooled, for the day is hot."

Tarkad's heart sank. Must he sit here and drink water while he watched this man devour an entire goat leg? He said nothing. He thought of nothing he could say.

Dabasir, however, knew no such thing as silence. Smiling and waving his hand good-naturedly to the other customers, all of whom knew him, he continued.

"I did hear from a traveler just returned from Urfa of a certain rich man who has a piece of stone cut so thin that one can look through it. He put it in the window of his house to keep out the rains. It is yellow, so this traveler says, and he was permitted to look through it and all the outside world looked strange and not like it really is. What say you to that, Tarkad? Thinkest all the world could look to a man a different color from what it is?"

"I dare say," responded the youth, much more interested in the fat leg of goat placed before Dabasir.

"Well, I know it to be true for I myself have seen the world all of a different color from what it really is, and the tale I am about to tell relates how I came to see it in its right color once more."

"Dabasir will tell a tale," whispered a neighboring diner to his neighbor, and dragged his rug close. Other diners brought their food and crowded in a semicircle. They crunched noisily in the ears of Tarkad and brushed him with their meaty bones. He alone was without food. Dabasir did not offer to share with him nor even motion him to a small corner of the hard bread that was broken off and had fallen from the platter to the floor.

Richest Ruminations

How different is the color of life when seeing it through the eyes of a starving young lad. Or from the perspective of a rich banker from a skyscraper. Or how about a man looking at his newborn son? What is your favorite lens through which you enjoy seeing life?

Dabasir said that he knows it to be true for he has "seen the world all of a different color from what it really is, and the tale I am about to tell relates how I came to see it in its right color once more." Any guesses what he means by that before reading the next chapter?

Blaming bad luck for your troubles reflects personal weakness—success comes from taking responsibility.

Day 29

THE TALE

"The tale," said Dabasir, "that I am about to tell relates to my early life and how I came to be a camel trader. Didst anyone know that I once was a slave in Syria?"

A murmur of surprise ran through the audience to which Dabasir listened with satisfaction.

"When I was a young man," continued Dabasir after taking a big bite of the goat leg, "I learned the trade of my father, the making of saddles. I worked with him in his shop and took to myself a wife. Being young and not greatly skilled, I could earn but little, just enough to support my excellent wife in a modest way. I craved good things which I could not afford. Soon I found that the shop keepers would trust me to pay later even though I could not pay at the time.

"Being young and without experience I did not know that he who spends more than he earns is sowing the winds of needless self-indulgence from which he is sure to reap the whirlwinds of trouble and humiliation. So I indulged my whims for fine raiment and bought luxuries for my good wife and our home, beyond our means.

"I paid as I could and for a while all went well. But in time I discovered I could not use my earnings both to live upon and to pay my debts. Creditors began to pursue me to pay for my extravagant purchases and my life became miserable. I borrowed from my friends, but could not repay them either. Things went from bad to worse. My wife returned to her father and I decided to leave Babylon and seek another city where a young man might have better chances.

"For two years I had a restless and unsuccessful life working for caravan traders. From this I fell in with a set of likeable robbers who scoured the desert for unarmed caravans. Such deeds were unworthy of the son of my father, but I was seeing the world through a colored stone and did not realize to what degradation I had fallen.

"We met with success on our first trip, capturing a rich haul of gold and silks and valuable merchandise. This loot we took to Ginir and squandered.

"The second time we were not so fortunate. Just after we had made our capture, we were attacked by the spearsmen of a native chief to whom the caravans paid for protection. Our two leaders were killed, and the rest of us were taken to Damascus where we were stripped of our clothing and sold as slaves.

"I was purchased for two pieces of silver by a Syrian desert chief. With my hair shorn and only a loin cloth to wear, I was not so different from the other slaves. Being a reckless youth, I thought it merely an adventure until my master took me before his four wives and told them they could have me for a eunuch. Then, indeed, did I realize the hopelessness of my situation. These men of the desert were fierce and warlike. I was subject to their will without weapons or means of escape.

"Fearful I stood, as those four women looked me over. I wondered if I could expect pity from them. Sira, the first wife, was older than the others. Her face was impassive as she looked upon me. I turned from her with little consolation. The next was a contemptuous beauty who gazed at me as indifferently as if I had been a worm of the earth. The two younger ones tittered as though it were all an exciting joke.

"It seemed an age that I stood waiting sentence. Each woman appeared willing for the others to decide. Finally Sira spoke up in a cold voice.

"'Of eunuchs we have plenty, but of camel tenders we have few and they are a worthless lot. Even this day I would visit my mother who is sick with the fever and there is no slave I would trust to lead my camel. Ask this slave if he can lead a camel.'

"My master thereupon questioned me, 'What know you of camels?'

"Striving to conceal my eagerness, I replied, 'I can make them kneel, I can load them, I can lead them on long trips without tiring. If need be, I can repair their trappings.'

"'The slave speaks forward enough, observed my master. If thou so desire, Sira, take this man for thy camel tender.'

"So I was turned over to Sira and that day I led her camel upon a long journey to her sick mother. I took the occasion to thank her for her intercession and also to tell her that I was not a slave by birth, but the son of a freeman, an honorable saddle maker of Babylon. I also told her much of my story. Her comments were disconcerting to me and I pondered much afterwards on what she said.

"'How can you call yourself a free man when your weakness has brought you to this? If a man has in himself the soul of a slave he will become one no matter what his birth, even as water seeks its level. If a man has within him the soul of a free man, he will become respected and honored in his own city in spite of his misfortune.'

"For over a year I was a slave and lived with the slaves, but I could not become as one of them. One day Sira asked me, 'In the eventime when the other slaves can mingle and enjoy the society of each other, why do you sit in your tent alone?'

"To which I responded, 'I am pondering what you have said to me. I wonder if I have the soul of a slave. I cannot join them, so I must sit apart.'"

Richest Ruminations

Is where you are in life right now where you should be—or where you are because of unwise choices?

Do you have the soul of a slave or a free man within you? What makes you think that?

Embracing the discipline of a free person can lead to respect and success, regardless of your circumstances.

Day 30

A FREE SOUL

I, too, must sit apart,' she confided. 'My dowry was large and my lord married me because of it. Yet he does not desire me. What every woman longs for is to be desired. Because of this and because I am barren and have neither son nor daughter, must I sit apart. Were I a man I would rather die than be such a slave, but the conventions of our tribe make slaves of women.'

"What do you think of me by this time?" I asked her suddenly, "Have I the soul of a man or have I the soul of a slave?"

"'Have you a desire to repay the just debts you owe in Babylon?' she parried.

"Yes, I have the desire, but I see no way."

"'If you contentedly let the years slip by and make no effort to repay, then you have the contemptible soul of a slave. No man is otherwise who cannot respect himself, and no man can respect himself who does not repay honest debts.'

"But what can I do who am a slave in Syria?"

"'Stay a slave in Syria, you weakling.'

"I am not a weakling," I denied hotly.

"'Then prove it.'

"How?"

"'Does not thy great king fight his enemies in every way he can and with every force he has? Your debts are your enemies. They ran you out of Babylon. You left them alone and they grew too strong for you. Had you fought them as a man, you could have conquered them and been one honored among the townspeople. But you had not the soul to fight them and behold your pride has taken you down until you are a slave in Syria.'

"Much I thought over her unkind accusations and many defensive phrases I worded to prove myself not a slave at heart, but I was not to have the chance to use them. Three days later the maid of Sira took me to her mistress.

"'My mother is again very sick,' she said. 'Saddle the two best camels in my husband's herd. Tie on water skins and saddle bags for a long journey. The maid will give you food at the kitchen tent.'

"I packed the camels wondering much at the quantity of provisions the maid provided, for the mother dwelt less than a day's journey away. The maid rode the rear camel which followed and I led the camel of my mistress. When we reached her mother's house it was just getting dark. Sira dismissed the maid and said to me:

"'Dabasir, hast thou the soul of a free man or the soul of a slave?'

"The soul of a free man," I insisted.

"'Now is your chance to prove it. The master has drank too much and his chiefs are in a stupor. Take these camels and make your escape. Here in this bag is raiment of the master's to disguise yourself. I will say you stole the camels and ran away while I visited my sick mother.'

"'Thou hast the soul of a queen,'" I told her. "Much do I wish that I might lead you to happiness."

"'Happiness,' she responded, 'awaits not the runaway wife who seeks it in far lands among strange people. Go thy own way and may the gods of the desert protect you for the way is far and barren of food or water.'

"I needed no further urging, but thanked her warmly and was away into the night. I knew not this strange country and had only a dim idea of the direction in which lay Babylon, but struck out bravely across the desert toward the hills. One camel I rode and the other I led. All that night I traveled and all the next day, urged on by the knowledge of the terrible fate that was meted out to slaves who stole their master's property and tried to escape.

"It was such a journey from then on as few men live to tell of. Day after day we plodded along. Food and water gave out. The heat of the sun was merciless. At the end of the ninth day, I slid from the back of my mount with the feeling that I was too weak to ever remount and I would surely die, lost in this abandoned country.

"I looked across into the uninviting distance and once again came to me the question, 'Have I the soul of a slave or the soul of a free man?' Then with clearness I realized that if I had the soul of a slave, I should give up, lie down in the desert and die, a fitting end for a runaway slave.

"But if I had the soul of a free man, what then? Surely I would force my way back to Babylon, repay the people who had trusted me, bring happiness to my wife who truly loved me and bring peace and contentment to my parents.

"'Your debts are your enemies who have run you out of Babylon,' Sira had said. Yes it was so.

"Why had I refused to stand my ground like a man? Why had I permitted my wife to go back to her father?

"Then a strange thing happened. All the world seemed to be a different color, as though I had been looking at it through a colored stone which had suddenly been removed. At last I saw the true values in life.

"Die in the desert! Not I! With a new vision, I saw the things that I must do. First I would go back to Babylon and face every man to whom I owed an unpaid debt. I will tell them that after years of wandering and misfortune, I had come back to pay my debts. Next I would make a home for my wife and become a citizen of whom my parents should be proud.

"My debts were my enemies, but the men I owed were my friends for they had trusted me and believed in me.

"I staggered weakly to my feet. What mattered hunger? What mattered thirst? They were but incidents on the road to Babylon. Within me surged the soul of a free man going back to conquer his enemies and reward his friends. I thrilled with the great resolve.

"The glazed eyes of my camels brightened at the new note in my husky voice. With great effort, after many attempts, they gained their feet. With pitiful perseverance, they pushed on toward the north where something within me said we would find Babylon.

"We found water. We passed into a more fertile country where were grass and fruit. We found the trail to Babylon *because the soul of a free man looks at life as a series of problems to be solved and solves them,* while the soul of a slave whines, 'What can I do, who am but a slave?'

"How about thee, Tarkad? Does your empty stomach make your head exceedingly clear? Are you ready to take the road that leads back to self-respect? Can you see the world in its true color? Have you the desire to pay your honest debts, however many they may be, and once again be a man respected in Babylon?"

Moisture came to the eyes of the youth. He rose eagerly to his knees. "You have shown me a vision; already I feel the soul of a free man surge within me!"

"Where determination is, the way can be found" Dabasir replied. "I now had the determination so I set out to find a way. First I visited every man to whom I was indebted and begged his indulgence until I could earn that with which to repay. Most of them met me gladly. Several reviled me but others offered to help me; one indeed did give me the very help I needed. It was Mathon, the gold lender.

"Learning that I had been a camel tender in Syria; he sent me to old Nebatur, the camel trader, just commissioned by our good king to purchase many herds of sound camels for the great expedition. With him, my knowledge of camels I put to good use. Gradually I repaid every copper and every piece of silver. Then at last I could hold up my head and feel that I was an honourable man among men."

Again Dabasir turned to his food. "Kauskor, bring me more meat fresh from the roasting. Bring also a very large portion for Tarkad, the son of my old friend, who is hungry and shall eat with me."

So ended the tale of Dabasir the camel trader of old Babylon. He found his own soul when he realized a great truth, a truth that had been known and used by wise men long before his time.

It has led men of all ages out of difficulties and into success and it will continue to do so for those who have the wisdom to understand its mysterious power. It is for anyone to use who reads these lines: *With determination, the way can be found.*

Richest Ruminations

Do you have debts to repay—not only financial debts, but perhaps a debt of gratitude to someone who gave you a second change, maybe a boss or family member who needs an apology, or how about reaching out to a neighbor who needs a helping hand.

Are you living as a slave to your vices? Your bad habits, or maybe your strained relationships?

You can be the richest person in your home, work, church, workplace, community, and everywhere you choose to be—when you see the world in the color of freedom.

LO, MONEY IS PLENTIFUL FOR THOSE WHO UNDERSTAND THE SIMPLE RULES OF ITS ACQUISITION

1. Start thy wallet to fattening

2. Control thy expenditures

3. Make thy gold multiply

4. Guard thy treasures from loss

5. Make of thy dwelling a profitable investment

6. Insure a future income

7. Increase thy ability to earn

ABOUT THE AUTHOR

George Samuel Clason was born in Louisiana, Missouri, on November 7, 1874. He attended the University of Nebraska and served in the United States Army during the Spanish-American War. Beginning a long career in publishing, he founded the Clason Map Company of Denver, Colorado, and published the first road atlas of the United States and Canada.

In 1926, he issued the first of a famous series of pamphlets on thrift and financial success, using parables set in ancient Babylon to make each of his points. These were distributed in large quantities by banks and insurance companies and became familiar to millions, the most famous being *The Richest Man in Babylon,* the parable from which the present volume takes its title. These "Babylonian parables" have become a modern inspirational classic.

THANK YOU FOR READING THIS BOOK!

If you found any of the information helpful, please take a few minutes and leave a review on the bookselling platform of your choice.

BONUS GIFT!

Don't forget to sign up to try our newsletter and grab your free personal development ebook here:

soundwisdom.com/classics